PREFACE

The science of psychology provides many elaborate ways of assessing the physical and mental characteristics of a person, but none of them can compare with graphology in easiness, thoroughness and quickness. You need only a written paper, say a letter to you from the person you want to assess and within minutes you can draw an accurate picture of his character and capabilities. Does a man has enough energy and good health? Is he sincere, trustworthy? Or is he a cunning and selfish fellow? Is your girl-friend sensitive, generous and affectionate or a gross selfish slut? All these and hundreds of other questions can be answered satisfactorily by a trained handwriting analyst.

An important thing about graphology is that it is very easy to master. I have tried to present the subject matter of this book in a specially planned way which makes the learning of the art and science of handwriting analysis almost a child's play. But the book is comprehensive and complete. A lot of examples have been given and many finer points explained for the benefit of beginners. My vast experience in analysing the handwriting specimens of men, women and children of every age, profession and from different nationalities has come handy while writing the book and made it authentic and exhaustive.

46, Novello Street Fulhom, **John Gillman**
London, S.W.G.,
England.

CONTENTS

CONTENTS

INTRODUCTION

Handwriting is the most powerful tool of communication and expression available for the human mind. Graphology is the science of handwriting analysis. It is science as well as art and requires a special skill for its interpretation. Graphology did not spring, full blown from a single mind in a single day. In the 6,000 years man has been known to communicate by definite symbols from earliest pictorial and cuneiform characters on stone and clay in Mesopotamia, Assyria, Babylonia and Persia, ther is no specific point in time or place where we can say, it is here man first sensed that these symbols might be an exterior manifestation of something more than human thought. We do know that ancient Egyptians held handwriting sacred, that as early as 1000 B.C. in China and Japan, a rudimentary handwriting analysis was practiced. Japanese scholars of the time judged that character conformed to the way a man traced his bars, according to thickness, length, rigidity or suppleness.

Sketchily, we know that as early as three hundred years before Christ, Aristotle and orator Demetrius Phalereus anticipated that handwriting reveals character; and in 99 A.D., Roman historian Guetonians made a skilful study of Emperor August's personality from his handwriting. During the Middle Ages, only the monks practiced the art of telling character from handwriting, but in the Renaissance, it interested such intellectuals as Shakespeare, who said: **"Give me the handwriting of a woman, and I will tell you her character"**.

The first book known to have been written on the subject appeared in Florence in 1662. Its author, Comillo Baldi, was professor of medicine, philosophy and logic at Bologne University. Using his treatise, practitioners went from castle to castle, analyzing lords' and ladies' handwriting. But by the end of the century, it has ceased to be a parlor game, commanding attention and support from such great minds as Goethe and Swiss Pastor Gaspard, Lavater, between whom an extensive correspondence on the subject was exchanged and later published. Graphology was brought to the status of science by two French priests : Abbe Mandrin (who later dedicated his life to the science) and his disciple Abbe Lean Hyppolyte Miehon. They published two treatise on Graphology 1. Systeme de Graphologie-1871 2. Graphology or the Art of Knowing Men by Their Handwriting.

Brilliant-minds like Balzac, Robert Browning, Maupassant (who wrote, Dark words on white paper bare the soul). Disraeli, Alexandre Dumas, Sir Walter Scott, etc. and many others became interested in this science and practised regularly to their use.

Lean Crepieux-Lamin (Disciple of Abbe' Meihon) took an important step forward when he established rules for Graphology which made it a real science.

He emphasized a basic principle and a warning, namely, that handwriting must be studied as a whole, not as so many simple, unrelated symbols. Why? Because human nature, seldom simple, usually is very complicated and contradictory. To be accurate, therefore, graphology must combine both analysis and synthesis. The latter is a study of the psychological relationship of signs which modify one another. For instance a handwriting shows the scriptor to be open the honest. May we conclude that he is perfectly reliable and trustworthy? The answer is no,—not if his handwriting also reveals that he is both excessively passionate and weak-willed, for there are classic examples of the 'good' man whose honesty crumbled before his overwhelming love for some designing woman. In espionage particularly, the type of individual is easy prey for the 'Mata Hari' breed of spy. And so, as Crepieux-Lamin has pointed out, each of us is the sum total of our various charac-teristics, and when those characteristics are in conflict, they must be weighed for their respective strength of weakness in counteracting one another.

Before elaborating on the considerable variety of information which may be gleaned from hand-writing, we should note that one thing that it does not reveal about the writer is gender. The reason is quite clear. Without being a sex deviate, a man can have some feminine characteristics, just as a normal woman may have certain masculine traits. As an example, let us say that a perfectly virile man possesses refinement and delicacy of feeling to the degree that it is a character dominant. His handwriting will resemble that of a woman. In the same way, a sexually normal woman may have masculine authority, daring and courage to a high degree. Reflecting this, her handwriting could be mistaken for that of a man. But this only adds to the proof that our characteristics make our handwriting what it is.

Application of Graphology in Daily Life

There are many applications of Graphology which would surprise many people by its scope.

Know Thyself

First and foremost, graphology answers the need to know oneself. It has been said that a man has three characters: the one he exhibits, the one he actually has, and the one he thinks he has. Few people can accurately discover all the truth about themselves without help, since it is obscured by a number of things, not least of which is the strong tendency to deceive ourselves. And while it may sometimes be easier and more comfortable to hide from the truth than face it, it is neither wise nor profitable, and often it is downright disastrous. Like the body, the personality can become sick, and it never helps to just let it go. Then there are the unfortunate sculls who suffer all their lives from terrible fears which are entirely unfounded; and the many who (unaware of their natural aptitudes and lacking the pro-fessional orientation) are square pegs trying desperately, and of course hopelessly, to fit themselves into round holes. It is bad enough to be misunderstood, but not to understand oneself is intolerable and foolishly unnecessary.

In Human Relations

It is self-evident that to acquaint ourselves with the real, underlying character of those with whom we associate intimately or in any to other way, is to provide ourselves with a valuable safeguard against heartache and losses of one kind and another. Marriage, for example, need no longer be a gamble when two people can discover beforehand what each is truly like. Family relation-ship usually are improved and friction reduced when understanding replaces emotional thinking and attitudes. Graphology can enable us to encourage worthwhile friends an avoid false ones. Parents can guide their children more wisely if they are aware of their innate tendencies; and they ought to know all there is new about a nurse or a babysitter before trusting that individual with their offspring.

In Business

Employers can avoid hiring dishonest, incompetent or badly adjusted employees. Conversely, they can avoid firing a potentially good employee who may be showing up poorly due to some disruption in his personal life which is only temporary. Thus humanely, a worthy person can be given the understanding, help and time necessary to put his world back together again. A graphologist also can determine the candidate most deserving of job promotion and can help orient people for work best suited to their particular skills. Much of the risk can be taken out of choosing a business partner, of extending credit or of making decisions which involve an economic trust.

In Psychiatry

All type of abnormality (from slight mental and emotional disturbances to Schizophrenia paranoia and sexual deviations) are discernible in handwriting, and this makes graphology a remark-able diagnostic tool, permitting the practitioner to go directly to the root of patient's trouble. It also enable him to chart personality changes under treatment, and thus to determine if he is getting the right results. Additionally, by shortening the time of diagnosis and perhaps of treatment the patient not only is spared expense, but he may avoid one of the harmful side-effects of psychiatric treatment, which is that prolonged self-examination and analysis of the most minute thought and act tends to turn a person upon himself until he takes interest in nothing else. This creates another unhealthy state in the patient which may be nearly as destructive as the disorder for which he is being treated.

As already mentioned, graphology is now taught in several colleges and universities as a part of the psychiatry course; yet many practising psychiatrists never heard of it and reject its use. These same doctors will rely on Rorschach (inkblot) test which cannot begin to give what handwriting does—and certainly not with nearly the degree of accuracy.

In Medicine

Handwriting is full of health clues which clearly reveal disorders of the heart, of the stomach, of the joints and of the nervous and glandular systems. It also reveals epilepsy, among other things. Geriatricians find grapho-pathology enormously helpful in their treatment of the aged, because it permits them to distinguish between ordinary senility and mental unbalance, between the normal physical weakening which comes with old age and actual disease.

The newest development in the area of pathology has been the detecting of cancer from handwriting, which a graphologist named Alfred Kanfer has been doing after thirty years of research, pursued at first in his native Vienna, then (after he had become a refugee from Hitler) in New York, where he has received aid and encouragement from the Handwriting Institute. Since the medical profession in notoriously slow to embrace radical innovations (and they are right to be cautious), doctors scoffed in the beginning, although they could not quite figure out how Mr. Kanfer, by examining hand-writing under a microscope, could achieve a score of accuracy between 70 and 80 per cent. The odds against doing this by pure chance are about one in ten million. For long time, Mr. Kanfer himself could not explain why cancer should manifest itself in handwriting or why it should show up three months and even years before it could be detected medically. Then medical research turned up data which suggests that there is a neuro-muscular deterioration detectable in malignancy patients, and this of course would affect handwriting today.

In Criminology

Criminal tendencies signal themselves in the handwriting, and many tragedies could be averted by advance warning, that would place twisted people under proper supervision for treatment. Hand-writing, of course, cannot tell whether a person is guilty, and no one would want it to be used as evidence to convict, but it can determine whether a suspect is capable of committing a particular type of crime. For instance, whether he might kill out of passion, out of fear of detection for a lesser crime, or from sheer pathological brutality. In other words, where several suspects are being investigated, it can point to the likeliest on whom to concentrate.

In Grapho-Therapeutics

In treatment of personality and character flaws through deliberately made changes in the handwriting offers a whole new field for the graphology. The possibilities for giving quick and effective help where it is needed are almost boundless in dealing with the myriad problems that grow out of character defects. In the case of children, where character is in the process of being formed, grapho-therapy is particularly effective and ideal. And this is true whether the child in question is "disturbed" delinquent or just an average youngster needing guidance to arrest undesirable tendencies and to develop good, sturdy characteristics to see him through life and permit him to make the most of his potentials.

1

A MANUAL OF BASIC GRAPHOLOGY

General Classification

SUPERIOR-INFERIOR

Superiority and inferiority in handwriting are judged by the degree of harmony or inharmony.

This has nothing to do with what generally is considered to be beautiful penmanship. Harmony is revealed by clarity, good balance and proportion, originality and the absence of extravagant movements of the pen. Any kind of excess breaks the harmony and diminishes the intellectual value, as a rule, if you find 'much too much' of anything, you will have an inharmonious handwriting. It may be too large or too small, too flourished or too banal, too heavy or too faint, too regular or too irregular, too slanted, and so on.

For purposes of reference, we designate harmonious handwriting as superior, and inharmonious handwriting as inferior.

According to whether we are dealing with the superior or the inferior, the significance of some signs and aspects will vary. To explain the reason for this, let us examine the shades of meaning in the word 'Pride'. On the positive side, it indicates self-respect dignity. But let it get cut of hand, and we have its negative aspect, vanity, conceit, pompousness. Almost any good trait can be exaggerated to a fault. The following brief table gives a few further examples of quick comparison.

Type	*In Superior HW It Denotes*	*In Inferior HW It Denotes*
Small	Good concentration	Pettiness
Light	Delicacy, spirituality	Debility
Fast	Spontaneity, vivacity	Impetuosity
Sinuous	Diplomacy	Prevarication, ruse
Disconnected	Intuition	Illogic

Figure 1, is an example of inferior handwriting. It takes no training to see that the movement, proportions and arrangements are graceless and unoriginal. The impression is of disorder, carelessness, vulgarity.

> We just wanted to let you know that we had a perfectly wonderful time at your dinner party the other night, the food was delightful

Figure 2, is a superb example of superior handwriting, since it meets all the requirements for clarity, balance, moderation and originality, without a single jarring note. The effect is both arresting and pleasing. You fell instinctively that the writer is no ordinary mentality.

> Ce qui fait de l'espérance un plaisir
> si intense, c'est que l'avenir dont nous
> disposons à notre gré, nous apparaît en
> même temps sous une multitude de
> formes, également souriantes, également
> possibles Même si la plus désirée d'entre
> elles se réalise, il faudra faire le sacrifice

GENRES

Each handwriting derives its distinctive aspect from its collective peculiarities. These fall into two classification : the *Fundamentals* and the *Accessories*.

Remembering that the fundamentals may be modified by a later examination of the accessories, the second step in analysis is to make a primary classification of the specimen handwriting according to eight basic genres, as follows :

1.	Slant	'defines'	Emotion (degree of expression or restraint)
2.	Base Line Direction	'defines'	Mood
3.	Size	'defines'	Vital power, opinion of oneself and of one's role in life.
4.	Continuity	'defines'	Mode, quality and coherence of thought.
5.	Form	'defines"	Inborn tendencies, originality, taste, individuality.
6.	Arrangement (orderly or disorderly)	'defines'	Sense of organisation and adaptability.
7.	Pressure	'defines'	Intensity, strength and appetites.
8.	Speed	'defines'	Rhythm of physical and mental activity.

1. SLANT

Emotion (Degree of Expression or Restraint)

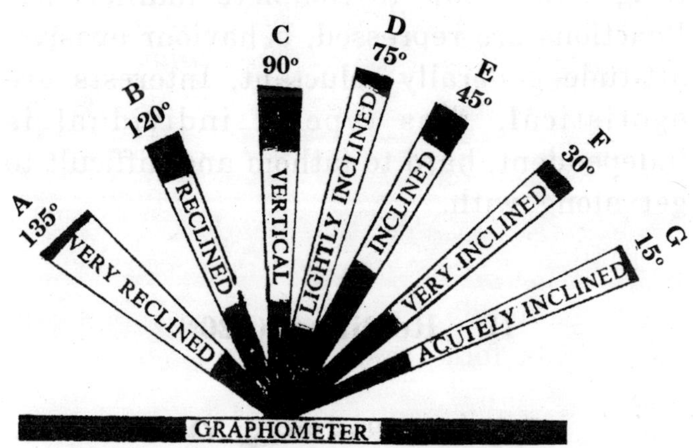

Place handwriting to be analyzed against the graphometer so that the base line of writing runs parallel to the bottom line of the drawing. Match up-and-down strokes with indicators on the graphometer to determine slant.

Mr. Manmohan Singh
P.P. No. - J-572825
c/o The High Commission of India
47 Independence Avenue

I. Very Reclined (135°)

Signifies : An emotional response that ranges from low to complete indifference. Reactions are repressed, behaviour evasive, attitude generally reluctant, Interests are egotistical. This type of individual is independent, hard to fathom and difficult to get along with.

II. Reclined (120°)

It is always such a
nice surprise when I see

Signifies : The introvert. A cold exterior marks inhibited feelings. Attitude will be diplomatic if handwriting is superior; if inferior, hypocritical and insincere. In general the backhand slant is undesirable. People who write this way are too reserved, indecisive not straight-forward and sometimes contentious.

III. Vertical (90°)

great lightness
and joy with one
on my journey

Signifies : The head rules, and the subject has complete self-control. Attitude is apt to be undemonstrative, independent, detached, even indifferent, and the keynote is cautiousness.

IV. Lightly Inclined (75°)

Jerusalem

Signifies : A normally sensitive and healthily emotional, well balanced person, when the handwriting is superior : when inferior, it generally shows mediocrity and conformity.

V Inclined (45°)

What a nice day

Signifies : An ardent, affectionate, amiable, very sensitive and emotional nature.

VI. Very Inclined (30°)

I saw Paul on Friday
Imagine it was a repeat!

Signifies : An intensely alive, ardent, passionate, responsive, susceptible, jealous individual, a brush fire.

VII. Acutely Inclined (15°)

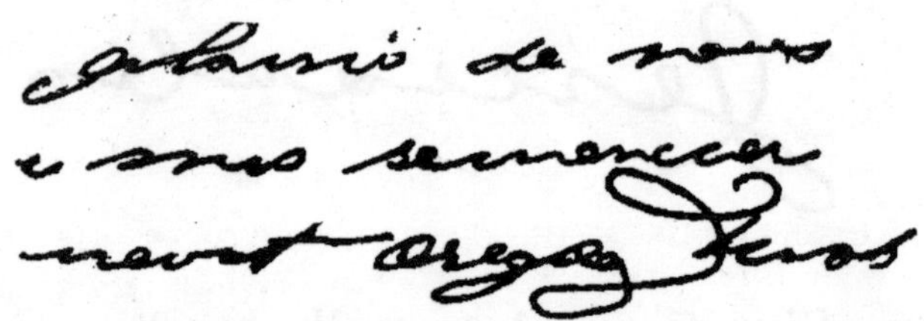

Signifies : Someone who is fervid, ardent, excessively romantic, passionate, jealous, easily offended, demonstrative (in certain cases, hysterical),—veritable volcano.

VIII. Constantly Changing Slant

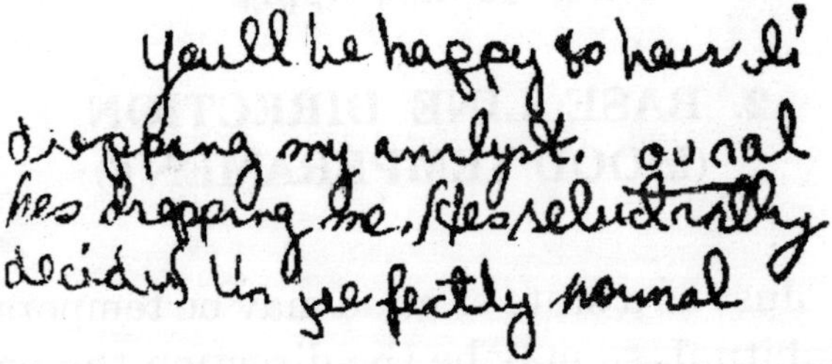

Signifies : General inferiority, an undisciplined, lazy, erratic, capricious, agitated, nervous, excitable, fickle, indecisive, nonconforming individual lacking in good sense or judgement.

The slant of handwriting, like the blood pressure can change temporarily under the influence of emotion. In a page of writing, it has been observed one section vary from the normal slant. When this happens, if the switch is to backhand from vertical or inclined writing, it means that the writer does not himself believe what he has written in that particular section.

One word more for 'slant'. Young people sometimes affect backhand during a period which corresponds to a transitory tide of self-consciousness, grouping and repression. It eventually passes, and the interpretations for reclined writing do not apply.

2. BASE LINE DIRECTION (MOOD/TEMPERAMENT)

Just as a state of mind may be temporary or habitual, so may be the direction the base line takes indicate either a passing mood or the natural temperament. It is advisable, therefore to have several specimens of handwriting execute at different times. In this way we can determine whether the slope of the lines is variable or characteristic. When several specimens are not available, we can sometimes tell from other traits in the handwriting whether or not the mood expressed in the sample is likely to be temporary or chronic. For instance, if all signs point to a normal, well balanced person, then a descending base line would suggest fatigue or illness or distress which naturally follows some loss or shock. Clues to the true nature of the situation will be found in the handwriting, and you will learn to pick them out.

I. Level

When the hand moves straight across the paper as if it were ruled, this indicates stability, conscientiousness, good balance, perseverance, equanimity, self control,—someone who does not readily yield to moods, who strives to be exact and to keep both feet on the ground.

II. Ascending

This type of writing breathes cheerfulness, enthusiasm, mental activity, energy, vivacity, initiative, hope when someone always write in this manner, it characterises, the optimist, an ardent individual fired with ambition. When it is not habitual, then it shows that the writer was reacting to some encouraging, exciting or happy stimulus that gave him a 'lift'.

III. Descending

I am having a very goo

If temporary, this indicates fatigue, discouragement or illness. If permanent, we have a pessimistic, melancholic, chronically morose individual and, possibly an alcoholic. If the handwriting plunges badly, the writer is dangerously depressed.

IV. Varying

They will cut down many group
of laurels and plant
potatoes in their stead
they will learn from

When the lines go awry which way in the same specimen, we have the impressionable chameleon whose mood can change colour with every whisper of thought or feeling there is instability, fickleness, indecision, vacillation, nervousness, excitability, emotional conflict and a lack of mental control and of discipline.

V. Wavy or Sinuous Lines

in Calif for several
years and I visit
you here also.

This points to instability, nervousness, inconstancy and (when corroborative signs of dishonesty are present) to deviousness. In superior handwriting, it can indicate diplomacy.

VI. Convex

I really want to play the
violin like you want me
to and I'm not looking

When base lines form an arch, it signifies a lack of perseverance. These people make a fine start when they set out to do something, but their energy soon melts and they give up easily.

VII. Concave

When the baselines dip in the middle like a loosely hung clothesline, it signifies the person who begins things hesitantly, unsure of his ability, capacity or strength, but with courage to keep going until the goal is achieved, in spite of physical or moral depression along the way. Thus it shows perseverance.

3. SIZE

(Vital Power, Opinion of Oneself and One's Role in Life)

I. Very Large

(Usually with Great Movement)

Bonjour de Paris

Signifies : Excessive pride, vitality, and a physically active, extroverted person who likes to be seen and heard. Tastes lean toward the ceremonial, the grandiose, the luxurious and the flamboyant, and these people are extravagant everything, restless and wayward. Dancers usually write like this.

II. Large

Highway

Signifies : An outgoing, nature, animation, courage, initiative, audacity, non-conformity, pride, self-satisfaction, expensiveness, altruism, generosity, imagination and an interest in big issues as opposed to details.

III. Medium

With the compliments

Signifies : Moderation, reserve, reasonableness, prudence, neatness.

IV. Small

Thank you

Signifies : Subtlety, delicacy, refinement, keen mentality, concentration, scientific interests and attention to details. In inferior handwriting it reflects the petty, exacting individual who cannot distinguish between what is not : the hair-splitter.

V. Very Small (Microscopic)

Signifies : Inhibition, fear, indecision, abnormal mentality.

VI. Large Capitals

(More than twice the height of small letters)

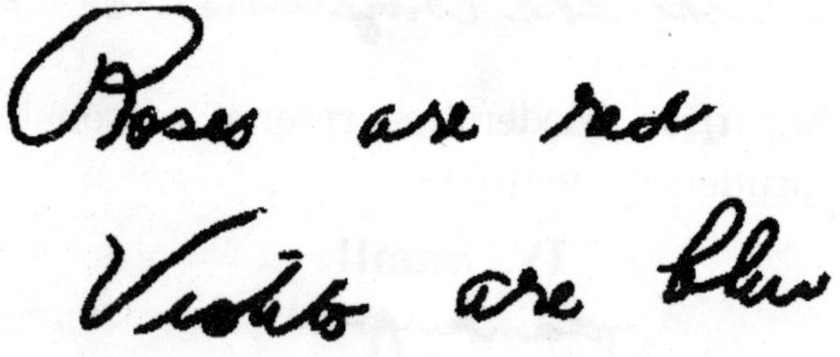

Signifies : Pride, vanity, self-esteem, conceit, arrogance, affectation, independence.

VII. Small, Narrow Capitals

for Delhi India

Signifies : Timidity and lack of self-confidence.

VIII. Capitals Slightly Higher Than Small Letters

San Francisco

Signifies : Modesty, simplicity, poise.

IX. Capitals No Higher Than Small Letters

new york city

Signifies : Humility, obedience, submissiveness.

4. CONTINUITY

(Mode, Quality and Coherence of Thought)

I. Disconnected Letters

(In Superior Handwriting)

Bonne Chance

Vive la France!

Signifies : Intuition, perception, intellectual and emotional sensitiveness, inventiveness, versatility, sharp imagination, tendency to mysticism,—someone who reflects before acting.

II. Disconnected Letters

(In Inferior Handwriting)

Hollywood

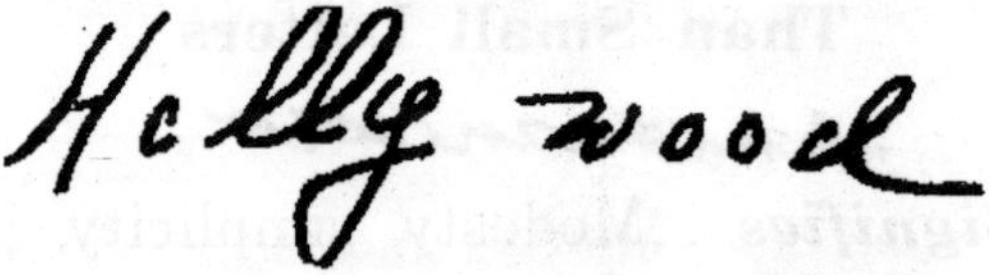

Signifies : An illogical mind, inability to follow natural thought sequence, impracticability.

III. Connected Letters

(In Superior Handwriting)

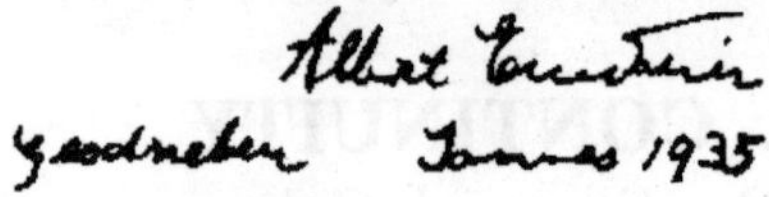

Signifies : Logic, method, power of deduction, an active and accurate mind, coherence perseverance.

IV. Connected Letters

(In Inferior Handwriting)

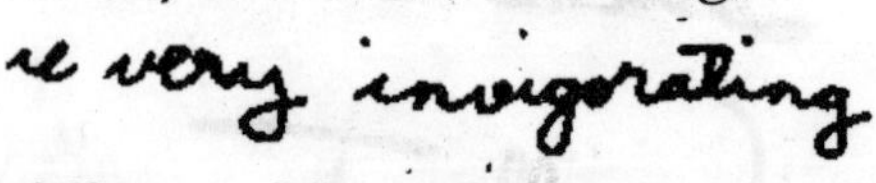

Signifies : Materialistic tendency, obedience to routine, deduction, pushed to extremes sometimes with false and absurd conclusions.

V. Connected Strokes of Equal Length

Signifies : Order, method, constancy, good judgement, reasonableness.

VI. Connecting Strokes of Unequal Length

Signifies : Emotionalism.

VII. Wide Connected Strokes

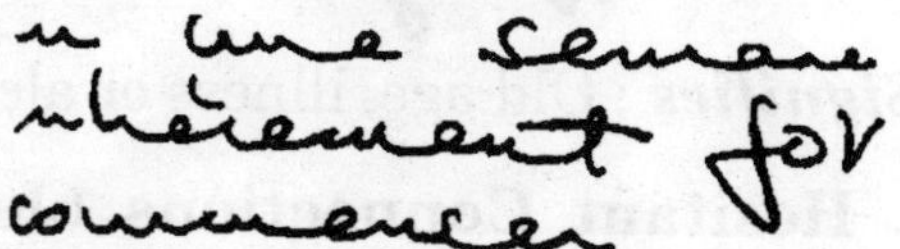

Signifies : Boldness instability, impatience to reach the goal.

VIII. Unusual Connections

any so very happy
someone to tell

Signifies : Originality, imagination, inventiveness.

IX. Sharp, Narrow Connections

This is a truly fine selection

Signifies : Tension, reserve, introversion,— a guarded, inhibited, ungracious individual.

X. Shaky or Tremulous Connections

Los Ang
Calif

Signifies : Old age, illness or alcoholism.

XI. Hesitant Connections (Jerky)

skin to feel

Signifies : Indecision, agitation

5. FORM

(Originality / Natural Impulse and Free Choice)

Each handwriting has its own distinctive form, influenced in part by the nature of the writer and also by his choice of style, which expresses his taste, originality and individuality.

I. Curved

with all things
you cheerful

Signifies : Goodheartedness, affection, adaptability, sociability, flexibility, harmony, aesthetic taste, graceful manner. The degree of roundness indicates to what extent these qualities are present, and when it is excessively rounded, it reveals child like naivete and submissiveness. In conjunction with light pressure, curved handwriting signifies gentleness, sweetness, submissive-ness, patience; also that the writer may be easily influenced, and unless careful, the resources and very life of these people can be drained in superficial pursuits.

II. Completely Angular

I am writing
aforesaid matter

Signifies : Firmness, determination, perseverance, tenacity, aggressiveness, energy, non-conformity, rigidity, resistance, irritability, selfishness, activity, harshness, prejudice.

III. Angular Above A Curved Base Line

the lecture was in
be interested to attend

Signifies : The bitter sweet nature. The writer under an assumed appearance of firmness, energy and practicality, is soft-hearted and susceptible, Aware of it and determined not to be 'patsy', he covers himself with protective spines like a porcupine, to keep people at a respectful and safe distance. Superior handwriting with pointed letters and a fluent base line also indicates a sharp, critical mind, good judgement and efficiency.

IV Garlands

M's, n's, v's written to look like u's, letters united by curved baseline.

my man is very much

In superior hardwriting, this signifies an open, receptive mind, adaptability, amiability, responsiveness, great sentimentality.

many nice things

In inferior handwriting, this signifies superficiality, fickleness, lack of precision, affectation, too much softness, a desire to take the easy, expedient way even if it means hypocrisy and deception.

V. Arcades

Upper portion of letters curved to resemble arches.

Arcades signify artificiality, affectation, love of convention and formality; also a desire to attract attention and to produce an effect. In superior handwriting (above) the writer may attract attention on himself by his creative talents, for instance, as an investor, architect of builder. He will also be amiable, pleasing and sociable.

In inferior handwriting, arcades reveal vanity, ambition and coquetry.

When arcades are combined with angularity, they reveal mental trouble and/ or criminal tendencies.

VI. Ovals

A's, o's d's, g's, q's open at the top at right side.

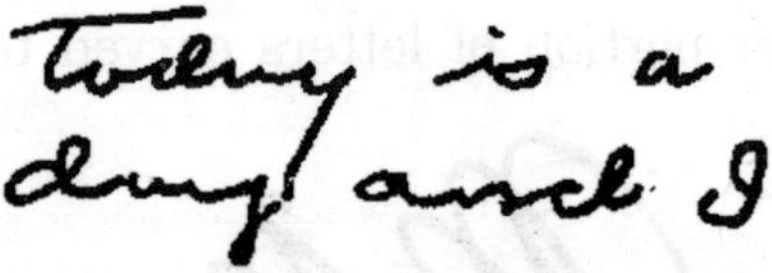

Signifies : The writer is an extrovert (outgoing). He is open, frank, loyal, sincere and conscientious. If the ovals are excessively open, the writer is ingenuous, expansive and assertive. He find it difficult to keep anything to himself, and may talk too much for his own good.

VII. Ovals Open on the Left Side

Signifies : An open, outspoken individual, but one who is also defiant and who does not talk about his own business.

VIII. Ovals Open at the Bottom

Signifies : The writer is false, dishonest and untruthful. This is typical of embezzler's script.

IX. Ovals Closed

Signifies : The introvert, the person who lives more interiorly than exteriorly. He is discrete, reserved, diplomatic, cautious, prudent and tends to secrecy.

X. Ovals Absolutely Round, Clear and Well Traced

who both go to a

Signifies : Good observation and memory.

XI. Ovals Closed and Locked with Loops

My family
Belgium
in this country

Signifies : Someone who is inscrutable, uncommunicative, complex, hypocritical and given to secrecy and lying.

XII. Ovals Open but Looped

Signifies : The type of individual who

sets traps. He is much too shrewd and dangerous to do business with.

XIII. Regular Form

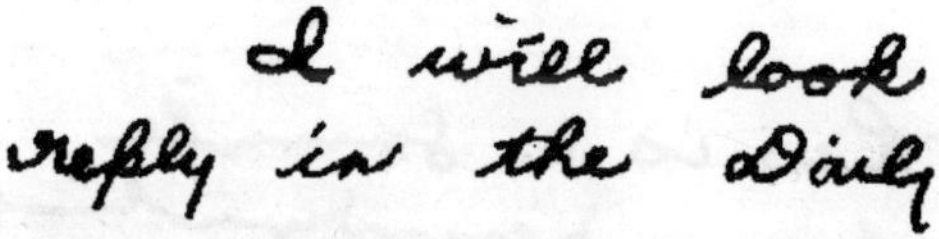

When letters are made neatly, more or less evenly and in regular form, it signifies orderliness, a good memory, efficiency, carefulness, self-control. Exaggerated, it points to the perfectionist, to conventionality and to monotony. When letters are attractively proportioned and harmonious, it shows aesthetic interests.

XIV. Irregular Form

Signifies : Disorder, carelessness, Exaggerated, it signifies slovenliness, lack of balance, neurosis.

Unequalness found in very sensitive and impressionable people's handwriting and often in that of artists and intellectuals.

XV. Natural, Simplified and Quick

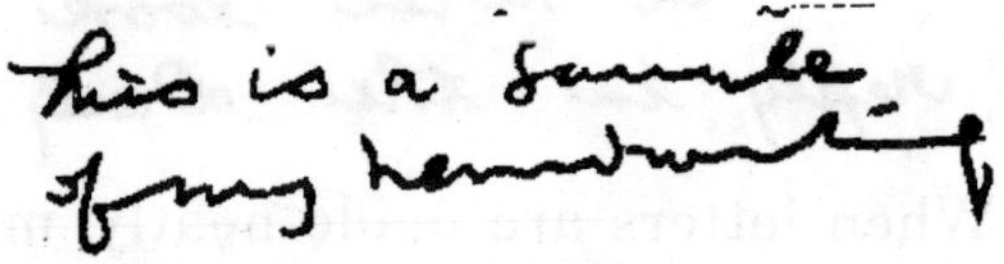

Signifies : A quick mind, unaffectedness, modesty, directness, skill and efficiency.

XVI. Fluent Form

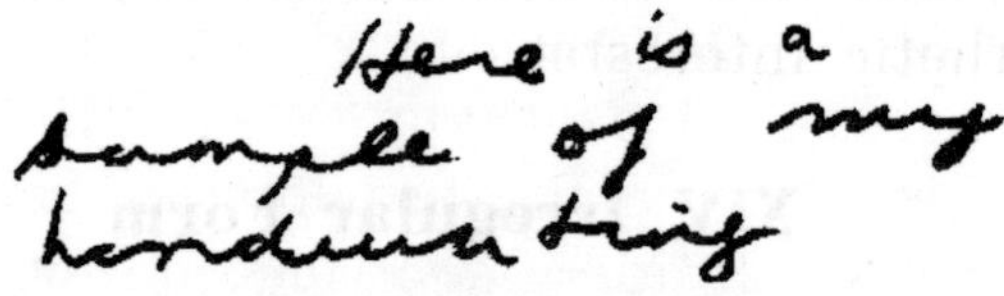

Signifies : Lucidity of thought, efficiency, responsiveness.

When form is the voluntary choice of the writer, he expresses his culture, taste, originality and individuality (or lack of these qualities).

6. ARRANGEMENTS

(Orderly or Disorderly)

I. Sense of Organisation and Adaptability

The manner in which a writer distributes his handwriting on the page tells us a great many things at a glance we can see whether it is orderly or disorderly, if it shows a sense of proportion and balance, if it is artistic and individual or routine and monotonous.

II. Well Spaced and Nicely Disposed

6230 Mulholland Highway Hollywood

Signifies : Mental balance and clarity, good sense of proportion and values, culture, order, carefulness, self-discipline, reasonableness.

III. Badly Spaced and Disposed

Thank you
very much,
love Pat

Signifies : Poor taste, carelessness, lack of order, of method and of discipline.

IV. Words Widely Spaced

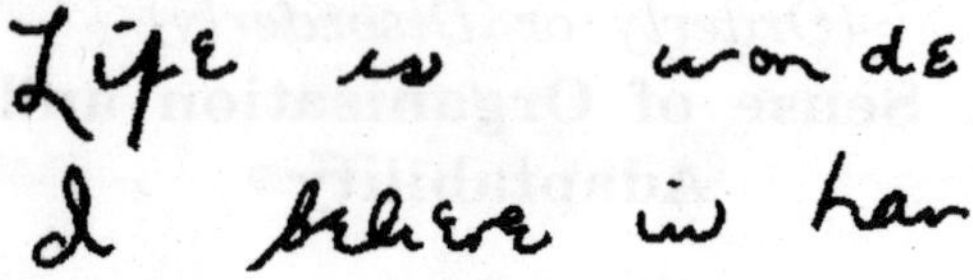

Signifies : Generosity, courage, independence. If too widely spaced : extravagance love of luxury, affection, audacity.

V. Words Crowded Together

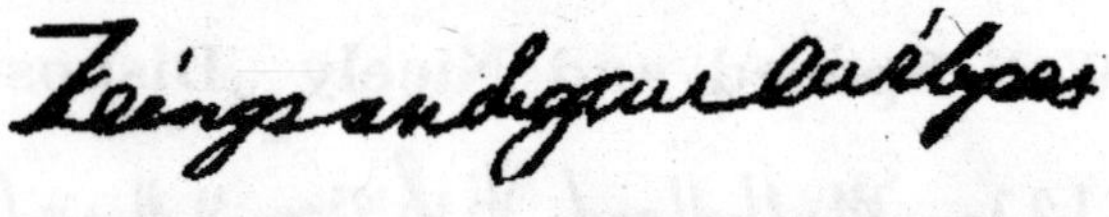

Signifies : Aquisitiveness, frugality. If very cramped : stinginess, narrow views, fear of risk, of action and of taking any initiative.

VI. Words and Lines Tangled

Signifies : Complexity, confusion, disorder, false judgement, inferiority, irritability. If very tangled, it also shows disloyality, agitation, incoherence, abnormal imagination.

VII. Legibility

want to improve
as much as pos

In superior handwriting, when both form and arrangement make for legibility, it signifies : high intelligence, clear thinking, an open character which has nothing to hide, and a desire to be in rapport with the exterior world. It also shows sociability, altruism, carefulness, conscientiousness, reasonableness, self-discipline, attentiveness.

really appreciate your
to help me and hope

In inferior handwriting, it indicates automatism, insignificance, ingenuousness, submissiveness to custom and convention. Meticulously legible handwriting may indicate the individual who, with something to hide and wanting to avoid detection, deliberately tries to "look innocent". But, some sign of what he is attempting to conceal will inevitably denounce him.

VIII. Illegibility

Although intellectuals and artists sometimes write illegibly, in general it is bad a sign. It shows, above all, inconsiderateness for those who must try to decipher it, but there also can be psychological reasons of guilt or inability to adjust to ordinary conventions and social customs.

In superior handwriting (especially when it is fast and spontaneous) it signifies artistry, aesthetic taste, disorder, nervousness, passion, unlimited imagination, impatience with routine, carelessness, nonconformity.

In inferior handwriting, illegibility signifies confusion, indecision, vulgarity, crudeness, inhibition, secrecy. When retouched and voluntarily illegible (to confuse and mislead), it indicates deceit and untruthfulness.

IX. Margins

In broadly general terms, the left margin corresponds to a starting point, the right margin to the goal.

When not dictated by the need to squeeze a message onto the only available piece of paper, the individual's choice of a left margin relates to the 'front' he puts up for the public: the right margin, to his real feelings towards the world. Whether or not the left margin is well maintained corresponds to how he succeeds or fails to keep up that front. A wide left margin reveals that the writer wishes to appear distant to other people; a narrow left margin, that he wants to seem close. The width or narrowness of the right margin shows how he actually feels on the question.

Other considerations which affect margins are thrift, taste and a sense of proportion. For specific interpretations, we look for corroborating signs in the script itself.

X. Margins Relatively Even on Both Sides and in Good Proportion to Size of Paper

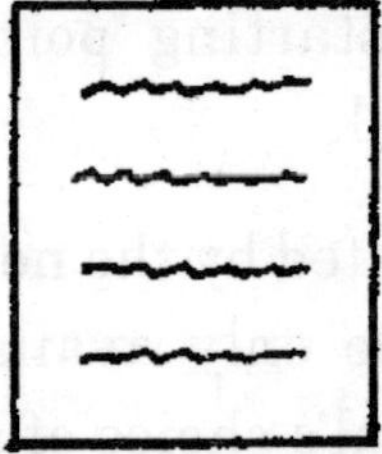

Signifies : A sense of harmony and proportion, good taste, order, poise, balance carefulness.

XI. Wide Left Margin, Disproportionate to Size of Paper

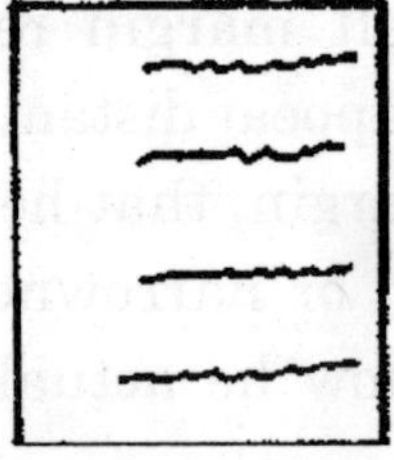

Signifies : The writer, for reasons of shyness, snobbism or pride, assumes an attitude of reserve towards others. If the margin is very wide, he seeks to be original and wants to be noticed.

XII. Wide Right Margin

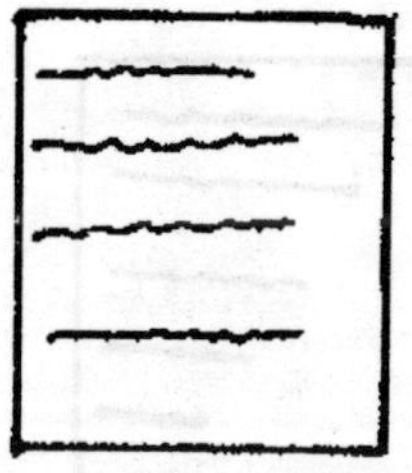

Signifies : Someone who actually is aloof from the world. It also shows a liking for the grandiose, immoderation, extravagance, wastefulness, fastidiousness.

XIII. Wide Margin All Around, Including Top and Bottom

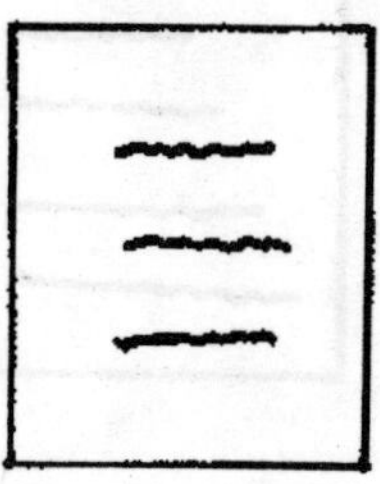

Signifies : The aesthetically or philosophically withdrawn individual.

XIV. Left Margin Widening as it Descends

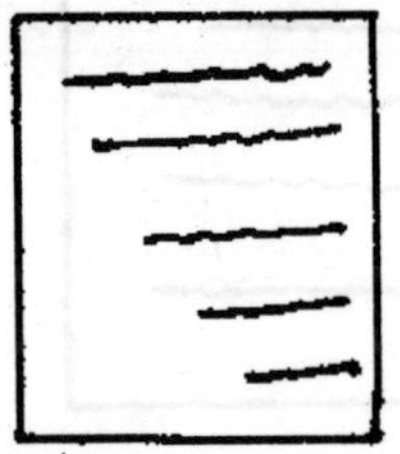

Signifies : Haste to make a point or reach the goal, ardor, optimism, nervousness. Also, that despite a need or desire to be thrifty, the writer cannot resist his love of luxury and urge to spend.

XV. Left Margin Narrowing as it Descends

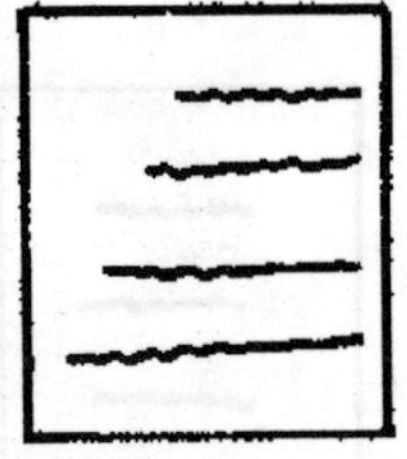

Signifies : Fatigues, physical or moral depression, lack of initiative and a sense of thrift which overcomes other consideration.

XVI. Narrow Margins Both Sides, or no Margins

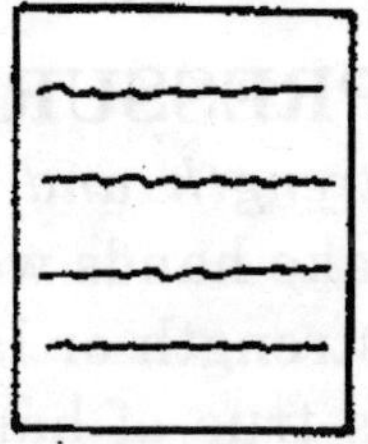

Signifies : (If other signs of thrift are present) stinginess. It also indicates acquisitiveness, practicality, bad taste tactlessness, lack of reserve. In outgoing people, it shows gregariousness, sociability hospitality, charity.

XVII. Uneven Margins

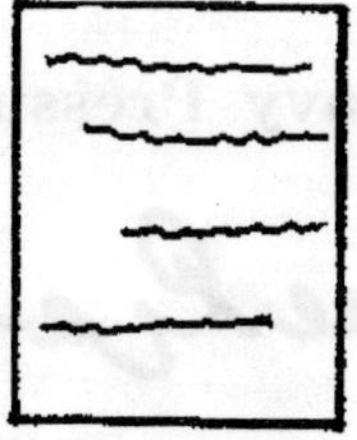

Signifies : Versatility, agitaion, lack of method, of order and of balance, carelessness.

A slightly irregular margin is more desirable than the too-rigidly-even one, for the latter signifies excessive self-consciousness, confirmity and that the writer watches his step out of some anxiety.

7. PRESSURE

(Intensity, Strength and Appetites)

When we shake hands we tend to judge a person by the strength or lack of it in his grip. The same is true of handwriting. The amount of energy exerted to overcome resistance of the paper to the pen, indicates the state of health, vitality, will power and sensuousness. Because certain type of pens write heavily without pressing it is well to examine the back of the paper where the raised impression made by pressure will confirm the appearance.

I. Heavy Pressure

54 rue Galilée

Signifies : Physical strength and activity, vitality, resoluteness, ardor, initiative, courage, self-assertiveness, materialism, aggressiveness, pugnacity, resistance, sensuouness.

II. Thick Muddy Writing Terminals, Angles and Curves Ink-filled

i love you Helen dear

I hope you will soon

Signifies : Sensuality, strong passions, violence, vulgarity, untruthfulness, sometimes bad sex habits or alcoholism.

III. Light Pressure

your column is very

Signifies : Moderate or feeble energy, low vitality, possible low blood pressure, refinement, gentleness, sensitiveness, timidity, submissiveness, little, or no " fighting spirit:. In superior handwriting it may indicate that interests tend towards the mental and spiritual. If light pressure is combined with shading, it indicates intuition.

IV. Even Pressure

handwriting, do

any indication

Signifies : Emotional stability, calmness,

reasonableness, clarity, carefulness, adaptability. When firm and even, it shows ambition, perseverance, self-discipline.

V. Uneven Pressure

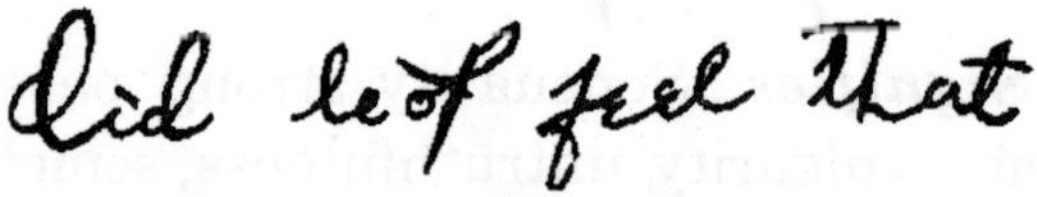

Signifies : Instability, indecision unequal will power, unsustained energy, an eruptive, excitable, changeable temperament, impatience, nervousness and inclination to worry. There may be such physical reasons as bad circulation, nervousness, glandular or digestive troubles. Generally, these people have little endurance.

8. SPEED

(Rhythm of Physical and Mental Activity)

In general, speed in writing signifies energy and spontaneity,—the latter interpreted as forthrightness and genuineness. Slow writing usually signifies low energy, hedging, caution, age.

To determine the pace the script, we can get a good impression by tracing over it to see if the hand, executing the same movements, can or cannot write rapidly. The following indications also will prove of help.

SPEED	
Faster	**Slower**
Curved Writing	Angular Wirting
Right Slant (inclined)	Left Slant (reclined), Erect
Connected	Disconnected
Uneven Pressure	Even Pressure
Widening Left Margins	Straight Margins
I-dots elongated into short dashes of commas and inexactly placed	Precise i-dots precisely placed
Easy, Natural and Simplified Forms	Awkward of Flourished Forms, especially with Left Turning Strokes which are unnecessary

I. Easy, Moderate Speed

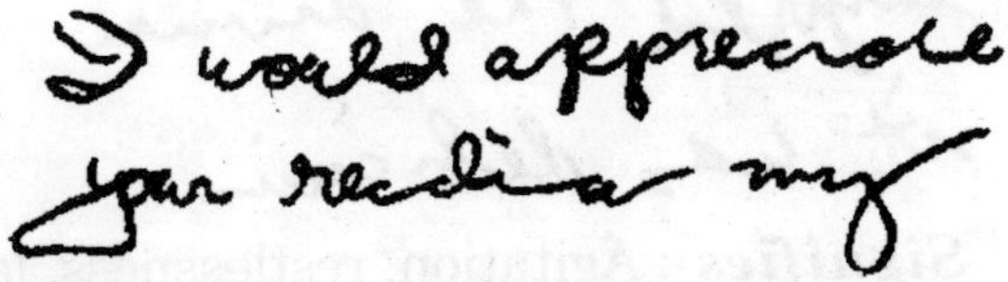

Signifies : Average intelligence, average energy, morality on a mundane level.

II. Rapid

Thank you very much —
I know nothing else
to say.

Signifies : Spontaneity, directness, dynamism, vivacity, culture industry, initiative, ambition, determination, adaptability. This is the person who gets things done.

III. Very Quick and Simplified

Signifies : Superior intelligence, intellectual activity, mobility, spontaneity.

IV. Too Quick and Hasty

(Not Fluent)

enjoyed the dinner
it was delicious

Signifies : Agitation, restlessness, lack of discipline, impatience , impetuosity, tactlessness, aggressiveness, possibly, mental troubles.

V. Slow

I enjoy writing letters,
meeting people

Signifies : A slow mind, cautiousness, fastidiousness, low energy, indolence, sluggishness, passivity, dullness, calmness, patience. If very slow and hesitant, indecision, procrastination.

ACCESSORIES

Having completed a study of the eight fundamentals (genres) which deal with the basic aspects of handwriting, we are ready to examine the graphic symbols grouped under the term "Accessories". As already pointed out, these are the signs which qualify, modify and confirm the basic symbols. They are the bits and pieces of evidence which must be considered along with the main evidence before a judgement can be rendered.

To be admitted as incontestable evidence, accessories must appear repeatedly in the handwriting, a 'book' or a misplaced curlicue, may be telltale; on the other hand, it can be due to a faulty pen, bad writing position, uneven writing surface or a jiggled elbow. For that reason, we must see either the sign or the movement reproduced several times before we can be sure it is relevant.

We find the accessories in 't' bars, 'i' dots, punctuation, capital letters, signatures, numerals, initials and terminal strokes, covering strokes, flourishes, upper and lower extension or, loops and in certain letters of the alphabet which lend themselves to graphic idiosyncrasies.

1. T-BARS

(Will Power, Active or Passive)

The letter 't' is by far the most graphologically important of the alphabet. Most handwriting movement is either in an up-and-down or circular direction. The horizontal 't'-cross, therefore, is a departure from the general rhythm that costs the write added exertion. How he meets this demand, determines the manner in which her bars his 't' s' and in it's many and varied forms, we read manifestations of the will, active and passive.

The will or the directed energy, is one of the most vital assets which a man can have. First of all, it enables him to do that which he wants to do by galvanizing him to undertake a project in a face of obstacles; then it supplies the drive necessary to overcome those obstacles and the determination to stay on curves until the goal is achieved.

Even more importantly, a strong will permits the control of self. A well disciplined individual can be neither misled nor enslaved by his appetites and impulses, nor does he have to repress them out of fear of the harm they may do, because self-discipline gives him dominion over them. A great many people deceive themselves on the subject of their will-power, and many who believe to be strong, are only stubborn. The difference, of course, is that 'will' is a positive force; stubborness is negative and usually evidences itself as resistance.

The person with the energy to do what he wants, is admirably endowed. But this vital power is not necessarily a gift which one must be born. It can be acquired, nurtured and strengthened.

But first let us examine how he will manifests itself in the 't-cross'.

T-Bar

Example	***Description***	***Significance***
	Normal pressure, evenly spaced each	Perfect balanced, calmness carefulness, complete control side of stem of thought and action
	Long and executed with heavy pressure	Energy, vigor, resolution, boldness, inflexibility
	Long and excessively heavy	Brutality, erascibility, tendency to domineer
	Light pressure, weak	Irresolution, timidity, moral weakness, despondency
	Excessively long	Enthusiasm, persistency
	Very long and thin	Vivacity, impatience
	Excessively short (in superior script)	Reserve and restraint of natural instincts Timidity
	Excessively short (in inferior script)	
	Ascending	Ardor, optimism, ambition
	Descending with light pressure	Resignation

Example	Description	Significance
	Descending with heavy pressure	Brutality, destructiveness, despotism, obstinacy, resistance, aggressiveness, assertiveness
	Placed above the stem	Excitability, imagination
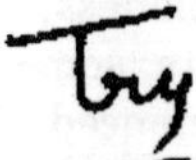	Above, very long, heavy and covering other letters	Dominativeness, authoritativeness
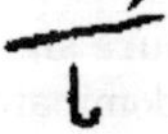	If very high above stem	Unusual imagination
	Low on stem	Conciliation, obedience, patience, possibly depression
	Post-placed (right of stem)	Impulsiveness, directness tactlessness
	Pre-placed (left of stem)	Procrastination, inability to make fast decisions, irresoluteness, cautious
	Curving or waving like a pennant	Fantasy, eccentricity, wit, pep, gaiety, charm
	Down-curved in form of candle-snuffer	Prodigious obstinacy
	Crack-the-whip	Vivacity, sign of the practical joker
	Hooked at either end	Tenacity, resistance, despotism, inflexible determination
	Beginning thin, ending thick	A temper that leads to violence
	Same thin to-thick ascending	Aggressiveness, pugnacity

Example	*Description*	*Significance*
	Thin-to-thick, descending	Brutality, cynicism, despotism
	Long and sharp at end like a hat-pin	Cruelty, wickedness, mockery
	Convex	Inhibition of instincts
	Cancave	Instability, fickleness, shallow interests, some one easily influenced
	Stem and bar made without raising the pen, in star-shape	Sensibility—a sure sign that feelings predominate the will
	Stem and bar made without raising the pen, final stroke a sharp whiplash. The feeling is that the hand draws to render a cutting slash	Indomitable, untameable character
	Looped	Tenacity
	Stem final incurved for the cross	Jealousy
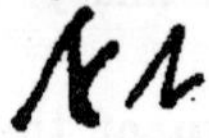	Cross replaced by a continuing upstroke	Fluency, efficiency, speed
	No cross and no substitute stroke	Carelessness, absent-mindedness, no will power at all, possible despondency

2. I-DOTS

(Speed, Sphere of the Imagination Intellect, Ideals, Aspiration)

The 'i-dot' is much more than the mere

speck it appears to be. Because it is an interruption to the forward movement, only the slow, careful hand makes it precisely round and places it precisely over the 'i'. The fast writer is more apt to make a hasty mark in the shape of a dash, comma or crescent, and to put it after the letter. Some handwriting may be so cursive that the 'dot' (which is not really one) is joined either to the preceding or the following letter. Thus, it is one means of determining the pace of writing.

The location of the 'i-dot' in the upper sphere also relates it to the intellect and aspirations. High or low, its position tells us whether the writer is exalted or down-to earth. And the more strangely the 'i-dot' is made, the farther the individual will be removed from the common place.

I-DOT

Example	*Description*	*Significance*
ı	Dot omitted entirely	Inattentiveness, absent-mindedness, carelessness, lack of order
i	Round, directly above the stem and firmly accentuated	This person is emphatic in all he says and does
i	Round and justly placed above the stem	Order, method, exactitude, poise, precision, conscientiousness, good memory and concentration

Example	Description	Significance
	Round and high the stem	Great imagination
	Muddy, looking like an ink-spot	Materialism, sensuousness
	Very light	A somewhat frail, amendable type who never tries to force his opinion on others
	Very high and generally light	The dreamer, with poetic tastes, lofty idealism delicacy, spirituality and mysticism
	Placed after the stem (post-placed)	A quick mind that looks ahead. In inferior scripts— impatience, impulsiveness
	Placed before the stem (pre-placed)	Timidity, cautiousness, procrastination, hestitation, fear of new ideas
	Very low, often lower than the stem	Constraint, embarrassment, illness
	In the form of a sharp accent	A lively, original mind
	High and dashed	Vivacity
	A reversed accent	Critical sense, imagination
	In either direction, but pointed like an arrow	Adds cruelty, and sarcasm to directional meaning

Example	Description	Significance
	In either direction, but club-shaped	Adds irritability (if very heavy pugnacity) to directional meaning
	Curved or crescent shaped	Vivacity, humor, love of fun
	Circle shaped	Interests in arts and crafts. Someone who takes to fads in an attempt to be original
activity	Dot joined to the following letter	Activity, a mind that works much faster than the hand and does not want to loose its train of thought.

3. PUNCTUATION

Without being of cardinal import, punctuation does serve to conform other signs, and so is worthy of examination. In general the rules for 'i-dots' apply.

Example	*Description*	*Significance*
; ?	Conventional, precise and firm	Order, carefulness and attention to details, clarity, prudence, conventionality
; !	Accentuated	Cautiousness, reasonableness

1977.—	Exaggerated and uselessly placed	Hesitation, lack of initiative, anxiety, pessimism
)iscal	Irregular, defective, neglected	Agitation, stinginess, carelessness, impatience possibly poor education
Sir--	Commas and periods replaced by dashes	Positiveness
Will you!-	Phrases or sentences framed by dashes	Mistrust, pessimism, a tendency to ingrained habits or beliefs
Sir,	Elongated commas	Exuberance, vivacity, enthusiasm
Ha!!!	Heavy or many exclamation points	Enthusiasm, dynamism
oh!	Light exclamation points	In significance a poor try at expressing unfelt enthusiasm
?	Interrogation point very large	Great imagination love of the marvellous mental exaltation, mysticism, romanticism, curiosity
now......	Excessive number of periods where three are usual to signify pause or transition	Enthusiasm
So how can	Too frequent, unnecessary underscorings	Exaltation, lack of good balance, an individual with strong irrational opinions
Get out	Heavy, irregular underscorings	Written in anger.

4. ALPHABETS

Besides the letters already discussed (ovals i, t), there are others of alphabet which are important because, they appear in such distinctly diversified form.

Letter 'd'

Example	*Description*	*Significance*
	Looped stem	Sensitiveness, susceptibility to flattery
	Final on upswept vertical stroke	Idealism, spirituality
	Greek d	Culture, literary taste
	Final on upswept right curve	Spontaneity, superficiality, thoughtlessness
	Loop ending with horizontal right turned	Ardor, imagination, spontaneity
	Final a horizontal left-turned stroke	An ardent imagination curbed by will power
	Left-turned final carried below the line	Pessimism

Example	Description	Significance
	Ending in a scroll or shell shaped convolution	Conquetry, vanity, flirtatiousness, desire to please
	Upswept final, terminating in a ballon	Imagination (the larger the 'ballon', the greater the imagination)
	Tall, upswept final looped very high	Authoritativeness, sharpness
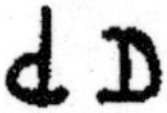	Printed	Artistic, good taste
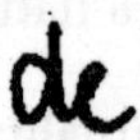	Connected to following letter	Power of deduction
	Varied form of the same letter	Versatility
	Big loop harmoniously slung to the left	In superior script, it shows logic; in inferior script, it shows a tendency to try to figure things out to be logical, even when mentality is lacking.

CAPITAL 'D'

Example	Description	Significance
	Exceptionally tall	Pride, vanity
	Stretched wide	Vanity, conceit

LETTER 'l'

Example	Description	Significance
love	Stick-like	Sensibility, intuition, a quick synthetic mind, that is, one which takes in all the elements of a thing and immediately sees them as a whole
learn	Tall upper loop or extension	Love for intellectual work and for making speeches, organizational talent.

CAPITAL 'L'

Example	Description	Significance
	Simple or printed	Culture or artistic taste
	Terminating left	Reserve, secrecy, obstinacy
	Descending curve at the end	Aesthetic taste, grace, gaiety
	No loop at all	Positiveness, reserve, materialism, practicality
	Base loop up-flung	Pride, self-admiration, boastfulness
	Base loop enlarged	Self-importance, vulgarity
	Resembling the Figure 4	Love of order, method.

LETTER 'm'

Example	*Description*	*Significance*
	Amplified	Intelligence, sensitiveness, taste
	Small and crowded	Timidity, narrow mind
	Rounded	Good heartedness, altruism
	Angular	Will power
	Too spread out	A bluffer
	Humps made like ovals or half ovals	Greed, materialism
	Up-and-down strokes covering each other	In sincerity, tendency to dissimulate and cheat
	Stokes broken	Parsimony, nervousness
	In garlands (U's)	Sweetness, desire to be kind and agreeble.
	The same, with a pronouncedly rounded base	
	A looped base	Affectation.

CAPITAL M

In the capital M, the first stroke represents the scriptor's ego, the second, his social status the third, other people. A tendency to aggrandize one or another of the humps show the relative importance placed upon the corresponding area of interest.

Example	*Description*	*Significance*
	First stroke highest	Pride, self-interest. If very high, arrogance
	Middle hump highest	Social ambition, bad taste
	Middle hump depressed	Dissatisfaction with job or social position
	Final hump highest	Envy of others
	All relatively even	Poise, highmindedness, intelligence, excellent taste
	Three humps instead of an initial stroke and two humps	Pride, thirst for honors and glory
	Initial stroke a hook	Selfishness
	Initial stroke a closed loop	Reserve, discretion
	Simply made, like an enlarged small m	Intelligence, good taste, sensitivity
	Curling initial and end strokes	Avarice

Example	*Description*	*Significance*
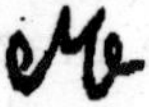	Ungainly proportions	Exaggeration, lack of taste
	Middle stroke plunging downward	Materialism, vulgarity, modiocrity
	Abrupt terminal	Energy, activity, precision, combativeness
	Final stroke plunging down and right	Pessimism, blues
	Final crossing back to the left	Prejudices, secrecy
	Final prolonged to underscore what follows	Selfishness, love of gossip, indiscretion (thus individual will confess very intimate things about himself)
	Humps wide apart with their heads depressed	Vanity, presumption, secrecy
	Too low for a capital	Dissimulation.

LETTER "p"

Both the small 'p' and the capital 'P' permit the writer to display spontaneity and a grace of gesture that reflects his artistic taste.

Example	*Description*	*Significance*
	Tall upper extension	Gaiety, affection, only average intelligence

Upper loop very high	Pride imagination
Lower extension curved left	Reserve, discretion
Lower extention ending in a left turned hook	Obstinacy, intolerance, exclusiveness, narrow ideas
Lower extension curved right	Quick mind, activity, spontaneity, boldness
Tong-like	Mental activity, precision, cultured mind
Simplified	A synthetic mind which can quickly assemble the parts into the whole
A single stroke	Vivacity, impatience, without a hump neglect, forgetfulness
Shell-like hump	Selfishness, positiveness, introversion
Ascending final	A taste for the aesthetic and poetry
Final ascending vertically and very high	Pronounced, artistic and poetic taste.

CAPITAL P

Example	*Description*	*Significance*
	Simply printed	Love for the beautiful
	Nicely curved, graceful and simple	Good taste, artistic ability, harmony

Example	Description	Significance
	Flourished and unharmoneous	Pretension
	Stem topped by a strange 'hat' with hooks	Intellectual curiosity, pretension, bizarre imagination
	A curlicue atop a stick	Pride, domineering personality
	Two curved simple movements	Intelligence, orginality artisitc taste
	Large balloned loop	Enthusiasm, imagination (larger the 'ballon' the greater the imagination)
	Simplified and swift	A quick, brilliant mind, Simplicity
	Terminal crossing left	Reserve, discretion
	Exaggeratedly tall	Pride, fatuity, pretension, snobbism
	A 'hat' very high above the stem	Idealism, inspiration, utopionism
	Made in one simple stroke	Imagination, originality vivacity
	Hump to left of stem	Timidy, strange habits

Description	Significance
Hump detached and right of stem	Mixture of narrow mindedness and boldness
Ending in a loop to left of initial stroke	A slow mind, hesitation
Ending in loop right of initial stroke	Initiative, activity
Set on a base	Artistic taste, also affectation
A wide swing on the leftward stoke	Cult of the past

CAPITAL 'S'

Example	*Description*	*Significance*
	Taller than other middle-zone letters	Imagination, pep, gaiety
	Undulating	Artistic taste, love of poetry
	Simple straight stroke	Artistic imagination, contrariness
	Comma-like	Impatience, vivacity
	Tied to the following letter	Continuity of thought, tenacity
	Final left-turned	Obstinacy, opposition to new ideas
	Ending in a loop under the base line	Tenacity with dissimulation
	German-form	Old fashioned.

LETTER 'v'

Example	*Description*	*Significance*
	Printed	Cultured mind, appealing traits
	Spread out	Originality, bizarre imagination
	Terminal covering the word	Devotion for the weak (an excellent sign)
	Final rears up and separates itself from rest of the word	A sign of revolt—the wish to break away from prevailing conditions
	Inturned terminal	Disillusion, tendency to draw back from people out of fear to be hurt again.

CAPITAL 'V'

Example	*Description*	*Significance*
	Simplified	Cultured mind distinction
	Terminal that covers the following letters or letter	Masculine instinct to protect and dominate (but frequently found in women's handwriting when some circumstances has forced a masculine role upon them)
	Sharp like hook terminal	Vindictiveness, meanness.

5. CAPITALS

The basic thing to remember about capitals is that they represent the way the individual wishes to appear to others. The exception is capital I (when used as a first person pronoun). Here, the individual unconsciously expresses how he feels about himself. When the other capitals are written considerably larger than I, the writer is putting up a front to hide a sense of inferiority. Conversely, when I is especially tall, it shows great self assurance.

Capitals are judged (1) according to size (the larger and more inflated they are, the greater the pride, vanity and desire to impress others); (2) according to form (flourishes indicate ostentation and flashiness, simplicity reflects modesty and genuineness; (3) According to originality and grace (which mean creativity, artistry and refinement of the writer).

1 Laura

2 Felise

3 Jack

4 Seneca

cyril anton

5

6 Charlotte

Mark Twain

7

8 Mutt

Dear Kathi and Paul 9

You must

10 Back

Fig. 1. Very tall (more than twice the size of small letters) and/or unflated or florished—signifies—Pride, vanity, self-esteem, conceit, affection, egotism, exaggeration, ceremoniousness, assertive-ness, arrogance, wish to be admired, love of luxury.

Fig. 2. Tall (about twice the height of small letters) signifies—Pride, dignity, ambition, independence.

Fig. 3. Tall & Twisted signifies—Non-conformity.

Fig. 4. Slightly higher than small letters signifies—Modesty, simplicity, reserve, poise and adaptability.

Fig. 5. No higher than small letters signfies—Humility, obedience, lack of self-confidence.

Fig. 6. Ornate and ungracefully fourished signifies—Bad taste, vanity, exaggeration, vulgarity, a gauche attempt to attract notice.

Fig. 7. Connected to following letters signifies—Altruism.

Fig. 8. An abrupt terminal—signifies a strong will power and tendency to be too brusque and blunt.

Fig. 9. In printed form—signifies—Simplicity, good sense of proportion, artistic taste, originality.

Fig. 10. Figure shape—signifies—Mathematical mind, method, precision.

6. BEGINNING AND FINAL STROKES

As children, we are taught to begin and to end a letter or word with a stroke, but except in the most unmature or conventional handwriting, they are either dropped or altered for reasons of practicality or as an expression of personality. In any case, these strokes (or their omission) are unconscious on the part of the writer; consequently they tell as much.

I. Beginning Strokes

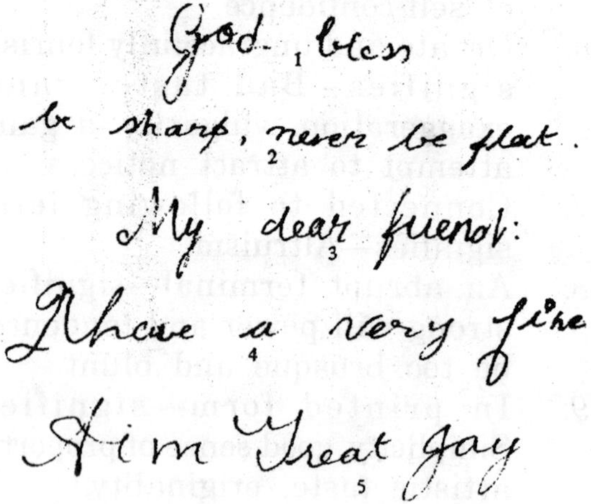

God bless
1

be sharp, never be flat.
2

My dear friend:
3

I have a very fine
4

Him Great Gay
5

Fig. No.	Description	Significance
1.	Omitted	Directness, efficiency
2.	Copy book	Immaturity, conventionality
3.	Hooked	Rapacity, love of gain
4.	Inturned	Selfishness
5.	Wavy and graceful	Gaiety.

II. Final Strokes

ai the 1 wee small hours
have been fine 2
you like the 3
Sicken or die 4
Just as rate 5

Fig. No.	Description	Significance
1.	Omitted or very short	Practicality, habit to economize time and motion, absence of sentimentality, acquisitiveness, directness.

2.	Ascending	Lofty ideals, aspirations, generosity, considerateness, kindness, spirituality.
3.	Ascending but terminating to the left	Writer yearns for some thing out of reach, lacking qualifiations to achieve his dreams.
4.	Ending in upturned hook	Selfishness, egoism, acquisitiveness
5.	Accentuated horizontal finals	Courage, perseverance, initiative, aggressiveness.

7 . Loops and Extensions

(Upper Middle and Lower Zones)

Upper zone deals with imagination, creative, spiritual qualities.

Middle zone is practical zone which deals with day to day activities level of consciousness.

Lower zone indicates sensuality, materialism, physical aptitudes etc.

The middle zone is that area of the handwriting, which accommodates the small letters having neither upper nor lower extensions such as a, c, i, m, etc. It is generally speaking related to the level of conscious, everyday things. The upper zone is the the area above the middle zone and accommodates the top portion of capitals and the upper extensions and loops of such letters as b, d, f, h, k, etc. It relates to spiritual, intellectual and creative qualities. The lower zone is that area below the middle zone which accommodates the lower extensions and loops of such as f, g, j, p, q, y & z.

When there are exaggerated and bizzare flourishes in the upper zone, it signals oddities and a mental aberration. Heavy pressure in the lower zone indicate sensuality. Distortions in the lower zone reveal sexual troubles.

I. Upper Loops and Extensions

1 will have 3 like to

2. sumpee 4 Oakland

5 double Purpose

Fig. No.	*Description*	*Significance*
1.	Tall	Great intellectual activity, idealism, aspirations, ambition, spirituality.
2.	Short	Moderation, little vision or imaginations, realistic practical viewpoint.
3.	Inflated	Exaggeration, egotism, boastfulness, vanity.
4.	Squeezed, compressed	Timidity, inhibition.
5.	Broken to the right	Fear apprehension for the future.

II. Lower Loop Extensions

Fig. No.	*Description*	*Significance*
1.	Long loops	Great physical activity, practical interests, love of pleasure, ambition.
2.	Long extensions	Maximum of physical activity and vitality, love of sports found in 75% of athletes handwriting.
3.	Short loops and extensions	Physical weakness, little interest in sex.
4.	Inflated	Physical vanity, pronounced sex nature, materialism, love of money, avarice.
5.	Broken	Secret apprehension about sexual and social concepts, conduct and eventualities.
6.	Triangular	Affection, snobbism, vanity, fondness for social formality, display of ceremony.
7.	Turned left instead of right	Fluency of thought.

2

SPOTTING DISHONESTY

It is the moral responsibility of the graphologist to determine the honesty or dishonesty of an individual whose reputation, image etc. may very well at stake. This should be done without any error and biased approach.

Fotunately, it is possible to be positive about deceit and dishonesty, and to evaluate it in all degrees, from functional diplomacy to outright fraud and thievery. Except in sharply defined cases, however, it is not easy to do. Dishonesty rests upon many factors, and to grade it, especially in borderline subjects, takes experience and a sound knowledge of human behaviour which cannot be reduced to simple rules.

In general, the handwriting of honest people has clarity, regularity, and a good, firm base line, that of dishonest people lacks firmness, has a sinuous or undulating base line, and is retouched. It may be illegible. On the other hand, inferior handwriting which is too painstakingly legible may reflect an individual who puts up a good 'front' to hide his shortcomings.

All generalities, however, must be accompanied by a word of caution; they are somewhat comparable to symptoms which suggest a diagnosis. It is necessary to probe for, and weigh supporting evidence. For instance, slowness (lack of spontaneity) is not sufficient in itself to characterize dishonesty, since there can be several blameless explanations for a slow writer, just as there can be for closed ovals.

Let us analyze what dishonesty is. It is not a single trait; in fact, it is not rightly a trait at all, but falls more under the classification of department. And dishonest department results, when certain moral and/or intellectual qualities are lacking in presence of such corruptive characteristics as a craving for luxury or power, love of risk and gambling, self-indulgence, over powering sensuality, intemperance, exaggerated acquisitiveness excessive, materialism or ambition, inconstancy, hyprocrisy, envy, aimlessness, selfishness, laziness, indecisiveness, prodigality, instability, weak will, wilfulness, rebelliousness, anti-social feelings, etc.

An important factor, therefore, in determining dishonesty or honesty (and one of the first things to establish) is whether the dominants (major traits) are constructive and positive. If so, they can outweigh minor faults. But if the faults are themselves, the dominants, they will outweigh any qualities which may be present in minor degree.

Thus we see that judging the extent of reliability is a question of evaluation and of balancing the " desirable" against the "undesirable". A knowledge of psychology is necessary, and a great experience and proficiency in analyzing handwriting also is essential before anyone may feel qualified to be an authority on this question. The rules for determining dishonesty are but guide points set up on the very tricky and dangerous ground which is human nature.

It was the late renowned Swiss psychologist, Max Pulver, who specifically classified the symbols of dishonesty, 'at least four' of which must appear together and very distinctly to allow a finding of dishonesty. In making the following, Pulver's method has been simplified for clarity.

I. Description and Significance

Please please write to me
immediately — as soon as I
get back to ~~the~~ office

Sinuous base line (the cardinal sign of dishonesty).

You are almost
dangerous
you can read

Ovals with loops and double loops (hypocrisy, secretiveness, dissimulation).

For my part I prefer
with people I contra
to seek to do things
who admittedly

Slow, hesitant motor sequence (lack of spontaneity).

Ovals open at the base, or traced in two parts (typical of the embezzler's script).

Any unnatural openings which break a letter into fragments, especially when openings at base or to the left.

Letters broken (torn apart) lower loops distorted.

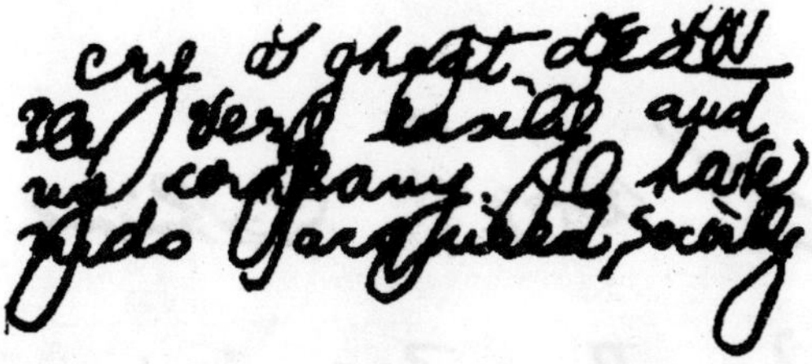

Words and lines tangled (disloyality, false judgement, complexity).

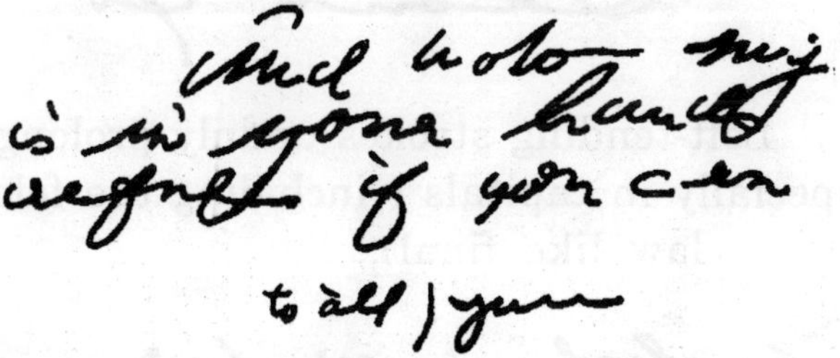

Misplaced periods (especially inside of letters).

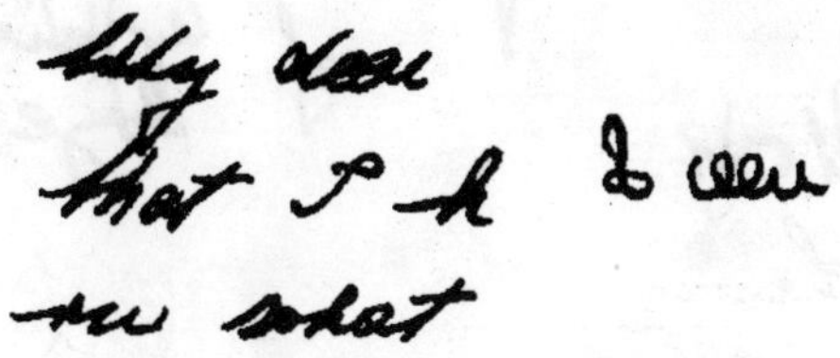

Covering strokes (up-and-down strokes written over each-other).

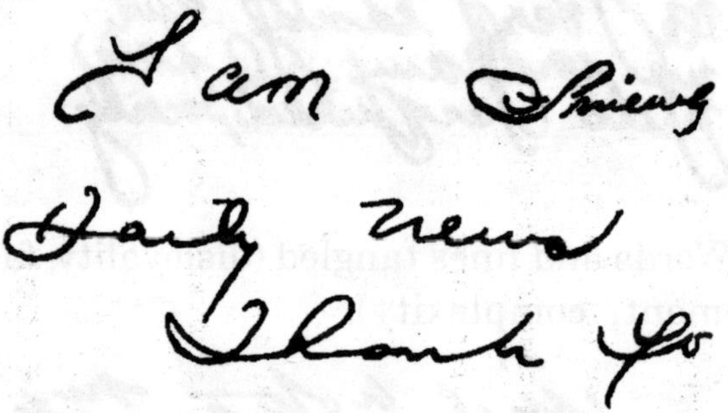

Left-tending strokes unduly prolonged, especially in capitals (including the felon's bitter, claw like final).

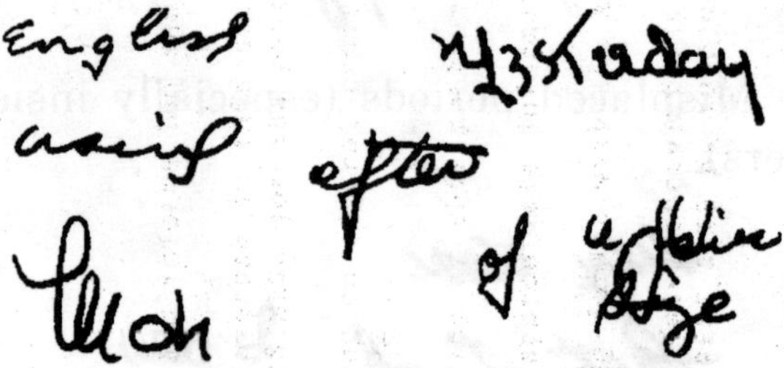

Strokes tuning left, when to turn to right is normal.

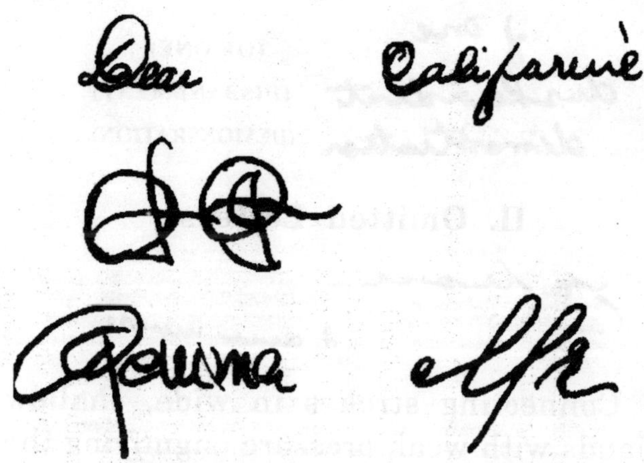

Initial and terminal strokes rolled up and complicated, especially in capitals (avarice).

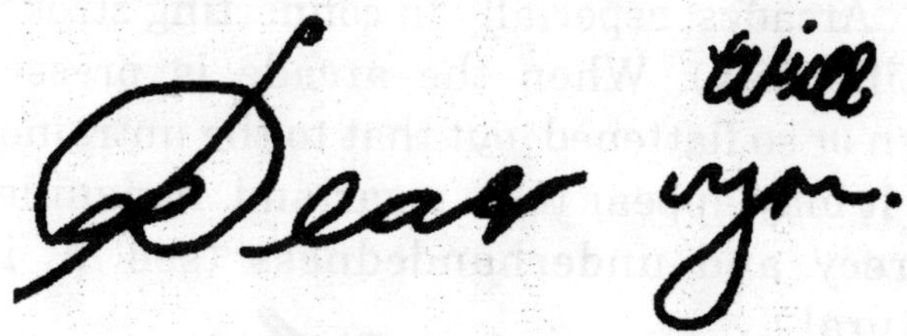

Frequent strange starts on initial strokes.

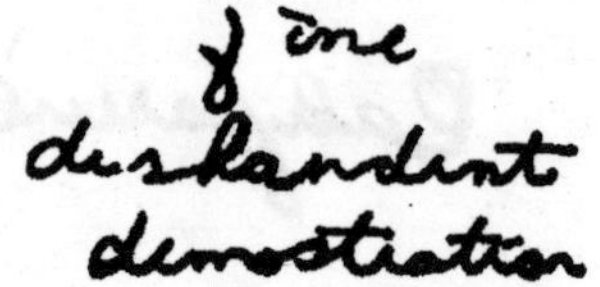

(OF ONE)
(DISBANDMENT)
(DEMONSRATION)

II. Omitted Letters

Connecting strokes in wide, shallow garlands with weak pressure (signifying the individual inclined to take the easy, expedient way and to reach his goal with reckless haste).

Arcades, especially in connecting strokes (artificiality). When the arcade is pressed down or so flattened out that to the untrained eye it may appear to be a garland, it signifies secrecy and underhandedness (see ‘n’ in ‘natural’).

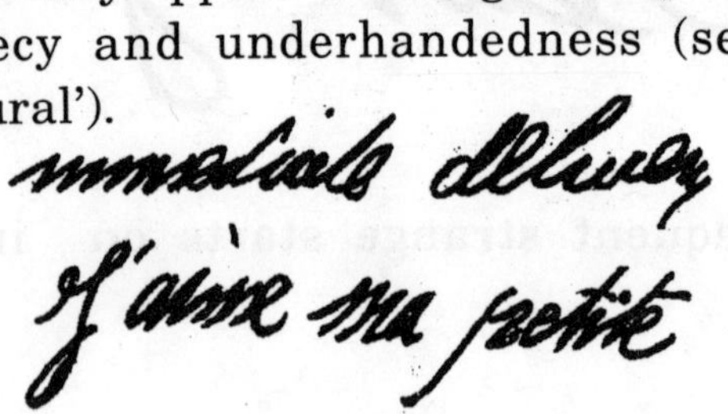

Arcades combined with angularity (criminal tendencies or mental trouble).

Oversimplification or alteration of letters to the extent they become ambiguous.

Corrections and retouched letters (except where done for improved legibility).

T-bars weak or non-existent (weak will power).

Looking forward to seeing you

from your loving
daughter
Elizabeth

Sharp divergence between signature and text.

15546

Numerals voluntarily distinct so they can be mistaken for other figures.

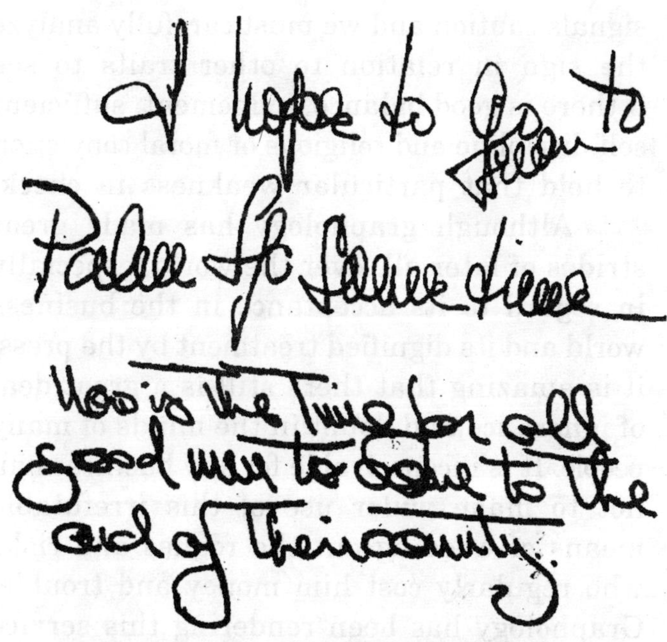

If none of the above signs appear in a handwriting, the scriptor is scrupulously honest and trustworthy.

To categorise a person into dishonest and unreliable one must have atleast four of the above listed signs. The degree and extent of dishonesty will depend upon the type of sign present in the script.

If any of them appears distinctly enough to be characteristic of the handwriting, it signals caution and we must carefully analyze the sign in relation to other traits to see if there is good balance, judgement, sufficient self-discipline and religious or moral conviction to hold that particular weakness in check.

Although graphology has made great strides of later all over the world, especially in regard to its acceptance in the business world and its dignified treatment by the press, it is amazing that there still is a great deal of ignorance and doubt in the minds of many people. It is inconceivable for any businessman not to make wider use of this irrefutable means of weeding out the rogues and risks who regularly cost him money and trouble. Graphology has been rendering this service for the past thirty five years, including that paragon of conservatism Lloyd's of London, along with its branches the world over.

Spotting dishonesty can be a vital tool for businessman before employing a person or making a deal which involves plenty of money or faith. It can be effectively be employed in partnerships and many other fields where honesty is the main requirement of the process.

3

RESULTANTS

As pointed out, it is not enough to know the eight 'genres' and the graphologist alphabet to be an able graphologist. Only a few fundamental traits (a very few) can be identified with certainty by a single graphic sign.

They are:

Trait	*Graphic Sign*
Activity	Speed
Depression	Descending Lines
Frankness	Open Ovals
Intuition	Disconnected Letters
Perseverance	Harpoon ending on T-Bars
Pride	Inflated Capitals
Prodigality	Too widely spaced letters and much wasted space on the paper
Sensitiveness	Accentuated Slant to the Right
Sensuousness	Thick, ink-filled writing
Vitality	Pressure
Will power	Firm T-bars that Cross the Stem.

Not only are all other isolated signs unreliable unless they are either substantially repeated or fortified by atleast two additional signs having the same, or similar, import, but the diagnosis varies according to the general characteristics of the handwriting, determined by whether it is superior or inferior and by the dominants. By dominants, we mean those traits, which stand out for their intensity and frequency. For example if you find great movements of the pen fall upper extensions, high t-dots all in the same handwriting, then imagination is a dominant trait of the scriptor, and it must figure potently in the interpretation of other signs.

Thus while each sign has its determinable meaning, its significance is only relative because, in combination with an other sign or signs, it may be modified or neutralised. And while graphology is called handwriting analysis it is both analysis and synthesis, the later being the psychological correlation of symbols. The interpretations drawn from this correlation of graphic manifestations are known as resultants, Defined in simple terms, they are 'characteristic behaviour', produced by combination of basic traits.

To illustrate how a resultant is determined, please examine the handwriting in the following figure:

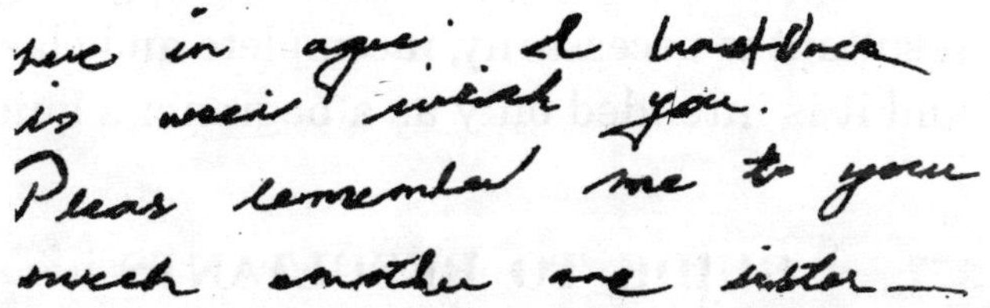

Note how the pressure is light and the t's are weakly crossed. This signifies a lack of energy and will. Note also how the sweeping pen movements and high i-dots reveal imagination. The psychological interpretation of this combination is that the scriptor is weak and unaggressive at the same time his imagination conjures up and enlarges upon the dangers he may have to face, causing him to be timid and fear ridden. From this, we find as a resultant cowardice.

The number of resultants is practically unlimited because of the variety of combination possible. This is why graphology, despite it is a science based on classified knowledge, requires a certain art of interpretation from the graphologist who should be solidly versed in psychology and have the faculty to look at a thing in all of its many distinct parts and see it as a whole the following list of resultant is necessarily, incomplete and elastic and it is intended only as a beginner's guide.

GUIDE TO RESULTANTS

Resultant	***Possible Contributing Factors***
Absent mindedness	Weak will, softness, obsession with one subject which limits interests in other things, capriciousness, unpracticality.
Adventurous-ness	Ardor, great energy, courage, ambition, taste for risk, curiosity.
Aesthetic taste	Grace, originality, sense of proportion, harmony.
Ambition	Energy, drive, acquisitiveness, materialism, high regard for and interest in self, ardor, eagerness for approval.
Amiability	Good nature, warmth, benevolence, native intelligence, indulgence, desire to the liked, harmoniousness, sense of co-operation.

Resultant	***Possible Contributing Factors***
Antagonism	Discordance, stubbornness, rebelliousness, selfishness, pride, spritit of contradiction. There are people who love a fight, whose nature craves a contest and who find stimulation is anger.
Ardor	Warmth, enthusiasm, imagination, prone to acivity, will power, energy.
Attentiveness good concentration	Intelligence, comprehension, will power, self-discipline, consideration for others, thirst for knowledge.
Automatism	Inertia, fixed ideas, weak will, indifference, discouragement, weakened mental tone.
Beauty-loving nature	Sensitiveness, delicacy, good taste, imagination, harmony.
Capacity for work	Energy, will power, ambition, good concentration, intelligence, ardor, constructive nature.
Cautiousness	Slowness, lack of self-confidence (to meet emergencies), negative imagination, weakness, indecisiveness, practicality.
Conscientiousness	Honesy, loyality, sense of duty, self-discipline.

Resultant	***Possible Contributing Factors***
Contrariness (spirit of contradiction)	Vanity, vivacity, stubbornness.
Conventionality	Mediocre intelligence, lack of originality, submissiveness, possible rigid early training, sense of imitation, cowardice, gregariousness (desire of mingle with and be like the crowd), eagerness for approval.
Courage	Will power, energy, daring, ardor, impulsiveness, self-discipline, altruism, sense of duty.
Cowardice	Too little energy, sick, fear fed by imagination, neither pride nor self respect but self love.
Creativity Curosity (Intellectual)	Imagination, intelligence, sensibility superiority, activity, assimilation.
Curiosity (Vulgar)	Inferiority, mental agitation, taste for intrigue, assimilation.
Decisiveness	Quick mind, will power, energy, courage, self-confidence.
Delusions of grandeur	Excessive pride and ambition, imagination, lack of mental balance, extravagance.
Devotion	Affection, altruism, sweetness, ardor, honesty.

Resultant	***Possible Contributing Factors***
Dishonesty	Unbridled ambition, rapaciousness, hypocrisy, untruthfulness, pliancy, self-indulgence, materialism, instability, supreme egotism, antisocial feelings, weak will. Either cowardice or boldness may contribute to dishonesty.
Disloyality	Dishonest tendencies, ambition, selfishness.
Dynamism	Energy, will, power, enthusiasm, pride, self-confidence, intelligence, leadership, originality, courage.
Envy	Selfishness, mediocrity, sensitiveness, materialism, greed.
Frankness	Honesty, extraversion, clarity, courage.
Generosity	Unselfishness, order, sensibility, altruism, spontaneity, an interest in large issues rather than petty details.
Goodhearted-ness	Sensitiveness, warmth, tenderness,imagination, empathy, softness, emotional nature.
High Spirits	Gaiety, energy, imagination, optimism, self-confidence, irrepressible order, expansiveness. animation.

Resultant	***Possible Contributing Factors***
Hypocrisy	Untruthfulness, insecurity, sensitiveness, nervousness, selfishness, cowardice, cupidity, complexity, false sense of values.
Imprudence	Eagerness, energy, lack of imagination and foresight, emotionalism.
Impulsiveness	Spontaneity without judgement, emotions rule the head.
Indecisiveness	Lack of spontaneity, unsustained will power, slowness, cowardice, imagination.
Jealousy	Passion, intensity, possessiveness, selfishness, sensitiveness, imagination, insecurity, pride.
Judgement, Bad	Mediocrity, gullibility, false sense of values, too much imagination, too much pride, over confidence....in fact anything excessive leads to bad judgement.
Judgement, Good	Intelligence, good balance, clearmind, sense of proportion and values, moderation.
Kindness	Delicacy, warmth, high sentiments.
Laziness	Very weak will, softness, selfishness, self-indulgence.

Resultant	***Possible Contributing Factors***
Memory, by association of ideas & by reason	Good deduction, quick mind, logic.
Memory (natural)	Intuition, facility.
Memory by sight	Good powers of observation, comprehension, penetration thus is evidenced in hand-writing by perfectly rounded a's and o's.
Mistrust	Negative imagination, anti-social tendencies, lack of self-confidence.
Moodiness	Lack of balance, depression, emotionalism, tendency to exaggerate both good and bad experiences, negative imagination, unsustained will power.
Observation	Keen perception, clear judgement, quick understanding.
Sense of passion	Vitality, order strong emotional nature, capacity for sacrifice, ambition.
Passivity	Low energy, weak will, dormant or weak mentality, lack of pride and self-respect.
Perseverance	Tenacity, will power, activity, imagination, patience.

Resultant	***Possible Contributing Factors***
Practicality	Moderation, self-control, head rules the emotions, sense of duty.
Procrastination	Weak will, lack of spontaneity, laziness, indecisiveness.
Prodigality	Generosity carried to excess, unrealistic optimism, ardor, an interst in large issues and no patience for details, emotions rule the head impulsiveness.
Protectiveness	Pride, sensibility, benevolence, empathy.
Prudence	Moderation, self-control, good judgement, intelligent, willpower, balance.
Rancor	A holder of grudges has tenacity, passion, intensity, susceptibility, hypocrisy, selfishness, negative imagination, lack of ideals, false values.
Rebelliousness	Anti-social feelings, passion, selfishness, intensity, violence (sometimes suppressed or frustrated), stubbornness.
Romanticism	Imagination, harmony, ardor, heart rules the head, aspirations, sensitiveness, grace, passions, optimism.
Self-confidence	Pride, intelligence, good balance, energy, decisiveness, optimism, firmness.

Resultant	***Possible Contributing Factors***
Self-consciousness	Susceptibility, hesitation, timidity, pessimism, negative imagination, softness.
Selfishness	Mediocrity, weak sensibility, greed strangely, we often find selfishness and good heartedness in the same individual. These are people who can be very generous, but who will inevitably extract payment of one kind or another—usually their generosity is aimed at buying friendship, love or blend loyality.
Self-sacrifice	The complete negation of self is abnormal, shows low energy, weak will, bad judgement false values, unmaturity and negative pride which feeds on the bitter fruits of sacrifice.
Stinginess	Cupidity, selfishness, pessimism, materialism, tendency to see everything in detail.
Superficiality	Shallow interests, suppleness, a tendency always to take the quickest, easiest way, false values.
Susceptibility	Sensitivity, vanity, gullibility, imagination, pride.
Suspicion	Imagination, naivete.
Tact	Imagination, sensitivity, empathy, self-control, good judgement, balance.

Resultant	***Possible Contributing Factors***
Temper	Lack of self-control, impulsiveness, passion, violence, impatience.
Timidity	Low energy, delicacy, sensitiveness, introversion, absence of pride and of self-control.
Tiredness	Mediocrity, cruelty, selfishness, caustic mind, rigidity, spirit of contradiction, anti-social feelings, passion, stubborness.
Vanity	Pride, ambition, ardor, self-love, poor judgement.
Vengeance	Extreme susceptibility, determination, pride, possessiveness, ardor, tenacity.
Versatility ingenuity,	Active mind, suppleness, curiosity, resourcefulness.
Violence	Inferiority, discord, ardor.
Wit	Gaiety, imagination, quickness, suppleness.
Worry, tendency to	Nervousness, pessimism, depression, negative imagination, superstition, lack of faith.
Zeal	Ardor, energy, pride, enthusiasm, desire for praise, sense of duty, passion.

4

HOW TO MAKE A GRAPHOLOGICAL ANALYSIS

In analyzing handwriting, the first considera-tion is to be certain that it has been written under normal conditions without any conscious effort. If it is possible to have two or three specimens from the same person written at different times, all the better for the accuracy of the analysis.

Never be influenced by the context of the letter. In graphology, language is unimportant and can, in fact, mislead you. Therefore a specimen written in French has been choosen to analyze together.

vous trouverez tout ce que nous avons
senti en regardant tout à la loupe,
avec tendresse et donc en lisant à haute
voix, en nous insurgeant contre le
moindre petit "gratton"
que pouvait déparer la belle surface
polie en disant ce que nous comprenions
qui ne peut être dû dans la totalité
des cas qu'à un mot oublié ou une
faute de frappe.

The supreme harmony which strikes the eye and dominates this hand-writing denotes, high moral and intellectual qualities. Let us check it, symbol, commencing with genres.

1. *Slant*—Very lightly inclined : a normally sensitive and healthily emotional, well balanced person.

2. *Base Line Direction*—Level : stability, conscien-tiousness, good balance, perseverance, equanimity, self-control, exactness.

3. *Size-Large (Moderately)*—An outgoing nature, animation, courage, initiative, audacity, non-conformity, pride, self-satisfaction, expansiveness, altruism, generosity, imagination and an interest in big issues as opposed to details.

3(a) *Capitals*—Slightly higher than small letters, modesty, simplicity, poise.

4. *Continuity*—Disconnected letters : intuition, perception, intellectual and emotional sensitiveness, inventiveness, versatility, sharp imagination, tendency to mysticism and to reflect before acting.

5. *Form*—Curved : good heartedness, adaptability, sociability, flexibility, harmony, aesthetic taste, an easy, graceful manner.

5 (a) *Ovals*—Here we have one of those instances which often confront us in graphology : mixed symbols. Some of the ovals are lightly open, some are closed (but without loops or complications). This indicates the 'ambivert' one who is both open and reserved, who is frank but diplomatic. This person knows when to speak freely and when to keep a discreet silence. Since we are dealing with superior handwriting, we can safely choose the positive qualities of both open and lightly closed ovals, and check them with other signs for verification. Thus we add : loyalty, sincerity, conscientiousness, diplomacy, prudence.

5.(b) *Regular Form*—Orderliness, efficiency, carefulness, a good memory, self control, aesthetic, interests.

5(c) *Fluent Form*—Lucidity, efficiency, responsiveness.

5(d) *Original Form*—Love of the arts, intellectual endowments, culture, imagination.

6. *Arrangement*—Well spaced and nicely disposed : mental balance, clarity, good sense of proportion and values, culture, order, self-discipline, carefulness, reasonableness.

6(a) *Word Widely Spaced*—Generosity, courage, independence.

6(b) *Legible*—High intelligence, clear thinking, an open character, sociability, altruism, carefulness, attentiveness, conscientiousness, reasonableness, self-discipline.

6(c) *Wide Left Margin*—No right margin. The wide space to the left can mean pride or snobbism, or an effort to be original to attract notice. However, in handwriting so clearly superior, reflecting modesty and moderation, we must look for a good and logical reason why the individual assumes a distant altitude when being warm, good hearted and sociable, he fools (absence of right hand margin) close to people. We can say then, that some circumstances (possibly his station or profession) compels him to appear reserved and to refrain from mingling with the crowd, which instinctively he should like to do.

7. *Pressure*—Although the appearance is heavy, the absence to deep impression on the paper shows it to be only moderately so. Since there is no accentuation in the lower zone (materialism, sensuality) we find physical strength, activity, vitality, resoluteness, ardor courage, initiative.

7(a) *Even, Firm, Pressure*—Emotional stability, calmness, reasonableness, clarity, carefulness, adaptability, ambition, perseverance, self-discipline.

8. *Speed*—Here again, we have mixed symbols and must make an individual judgement. While disconnected letters, even pressure, straight margins and some left-turning strokes lessen the speed, there is too much vitality evident in this handwriting for it to be slow or even moderate. From the general tone, then, we conclude that it is more repid than

slow, and shows spontaneity, dynamism, vivacity, culture, industry, drive initiative, determination ambition adaptability.

9. *T-bars*—Normal pressure, evenly spaced each side of stem : perfect balance, calmness, carefulness, complete control of thought and action. We also find quite a few short 't-bars' which indicate reserve and restraint of natural instincts (which bears act out margin findings, 6-c).

10. *I-dots*—Tend in general to be round and justly placed above the stem : order method, exactitude, poise precision, conscientiousness, good memory and concentration. Several dots are high, however, indicating imagination. And several are to the right of the stem, reflecting quick that looks ahead.

11. *Punctuation*—Convetional and firm : order, carefulness, attention to details, clarity, prudence, conventionality.

12. *Capitals*—We already have covered size. As to form, they are well proportioned and

graceful: intelligence, taste, and they are printed : simplicity, good sense of proportion, artistic taste, originality. Some of the capitals are connected to following letters, and this gives us altruism.

13. *Beginning Strokes Omitted*—Directness, efficiency.

14. *Final Strokes Generally Omitted*—Practicality, habit to economize time and motion, absence of sentimentality, acquisitiveness, directness. Some final strokes are short and (slightly) club-shaped: resoluteness, assertiveness, independence. The fact that there are no ' selfish' hooks on either beginning or final strokes, supports the 'altruism' found in item

15. *Both Upper and Lower Extensions*—Tend to be simple, moderate and neither inflated nor compressed; and none of the three zones is over-emphasized. This indicates inner harmony, moderation and a happy balance between the three spheres : (1) Intellectual and spiritual, (2) practical and (3) physical and material.

16. *Small 'd's' with Looped Stems*—Sensitiveness, susceptibility to flattery; angular 'm's' : will power; comma like 's's' : impatience, vivacity; S tied to following letter (as in 'tendresse', 'aussi', 'possible'). Continuity of thought, tenacity; printed 'v' and 'V': Cultured mind, appealing traits, distinction.

17. *Signature—(Not shown)*—is identical to the text, moderation, a clear thinker; and it bears a horizontal underscore : pride self-confidence.

We shall now determine which traits are sufficiently repeated and confirmed to be certain. Those which stand out (the dominants) are :

(i) Good mental and emotional balance, poise and harmony.

(ii) Order, method, exactness, efficiency and industry.

(iii) Lucidity and intellectual activity.

(iv) Culture and aesthetic taste.

Traits determinable by a single symbol are:

Activity
Frankness
Intuition
Vitality
Will Power

Other traits confirmed by repetition and / or by resultants :

Ardor
Amiability
Sociability
Easy (graceful manner)
Sensitivity (Intellectual and Emotional)
Distinction
Honesty
Sincerity
Loyalty
Devotion
Directness
Conscientiousness
Protectivenes
Good heartedness
Prudence
Altruism
Generosity
Self-confidence
Pride
Modesty
Simplicity
Susceptibility to flattery.

Dynamism
Strength
Drive
Resoluteness
Decisiveness
Initiative
Independence
Ambition
Courage
Perseverance
Tenacity
Self-discipline
Capacity for work

Practicality
Moderation
Reasonableness issues
Reserve
Adaptability

Flexibility
Diplomacy
Tact

Reflectiveness
Observation
Concentration
Application
Memory
Imagination
Originality
Creativity
Beauty- loving-nature
Good judgement
Sense of values
Interest in big

SUMMARY

It is evident that the gentleman who has written this specimen has high degree of intelligence, lucidity, culture, judgement and moral elegance with such outstanding qualities/combined with forcefulness, activity, decisiveness, self-discipline, poise, honest, prudence, imagination, originality, and initiative, he is a natural leader of men who, sure of himself, goes his own way courageoúsly, immutable in his principles, yet supple, just kind, generous and tactful in all his relationships.

In love, he is ardent, virile, sincere, loyal, devoted and delicate.

What he thinks, says and does always is in complete harmony; and it is due as much to this admirable harmony and perfect balance as it is to his strong will power, conscientiousness and self-discipline, that he has been able to adapt himself to handling practical matters and can buckle down to details when necessary, although his natural interest is in big issues, in the aesthetic and the cultural.

Let this man assume a task—any task—and you may rest assured it will be done intelligently, expeditiously and to the best of his very great ability. It would be impossible for him to disappoint anyone who has depended on him, or to fall short of his own exacting standards.

Since it is all too rare to find so superior and dynamic a man, it follows that he must hold a position of great responsibility and trust. It is possible that there is something about this position which has required him to curb his normal friendliness, to hold himself aloof from the crowd and to restrain his spontaneity. But beneath his reserve, we find that altruism and a love of his fellowman run deep and strong.

His pronounced sensitivity and intuition guide him in all he does, and he knows instinctively what he must do, as well as how and when to do it. He "feels" : people judges them on first contact, and seldom errs.

His self-confidence and pride are more than justified. The only fault to be found in this most remarkable gentleman is a slight weakness for flattery and praise. But everyone must be allowed some flaw to prove himself human. And this tendency toward self-satisfaction never gets out of hand. Let him warm with pleasure over a complimcnts,— with his nct brcath his good balance and down-to-earthness always remind him to be modest.

* * * *

At the opposite pole is the handwriting in (Fig..........). The confusion, inconsistencies, lack of clarity, the tastelessness and discordant appearance make it a very good specimen of 'inferior' (inharmonious) script. We shall analyse it together.

1. *Slant*—Constantly changing : an undisciplined, lazy erratic, capricious, agitate, nervous, excitable, fickle, indecisive, non-conforming individual, lacking in good sense or judgement. This handwriting actually staggers, taking first one direction, then another, every few letters. The writer is

tormented by emotional conflicts and is mentally unbalanced.

2. *Base Line Direction*—Sinuous (although writing on ruled paper, the writer could not stay on the lines) : instability, nervousness, inconstancy, deviousness.

3. *Size*—Varies from small cramped letters to large ones and even some that are blown up like ballons. This simply indicates that there is absolutely no sense of proportion and balance.

3(a) *Capitals*—Large : pride, vanity, self-esteem, conceit, arrogance, affectation, independence.

4. *Continuity*—Connected : materialistic tendency, obedience to routine, deduction pushed to extremes, sometimes with false absurd conclusions.

4(a) *Unequal Connecting Strokes*—Emotionalism (actually, the connection jerk and jump, indicating serious nervousness).

5. *Form—Haphazard*—We find garlands : super-ficiality, fickleness, lack of precision, affectation, a desire to take the easy, expedient way even if it means deception, and arcades : vanity, ambition, coquetry. The fact that both arcades and angular forms are present is another evidence of mental trouble and/or of dishonesty.

5(a) *Ovals*—Here again we have an assortment, but they tend in general to be closed and locked with loops : someone inscrutable, uncommunicative, complex, hypocritical and given to secrecy and lying.

5(b) *Irregular Form*—Disorder, carelessness, slovenliness, lack of balance neurosis.

6. *Arrangement*—Badly spaced and disposed: poor taste, carelessness, lack of order and disipline.

6 (a) *There is Also Same Tangling*—Complexity, confusion, disorder, false judgement, inferiority, irritability.

6(b) *Illegibility*—Confusion, indecision, vulgarity, crudeness, inhibitions, secrecy.

6(c) *Margins*—None : stinginess, acquisitiveness, practicality bad taste, tactlessness, lack of reserve.

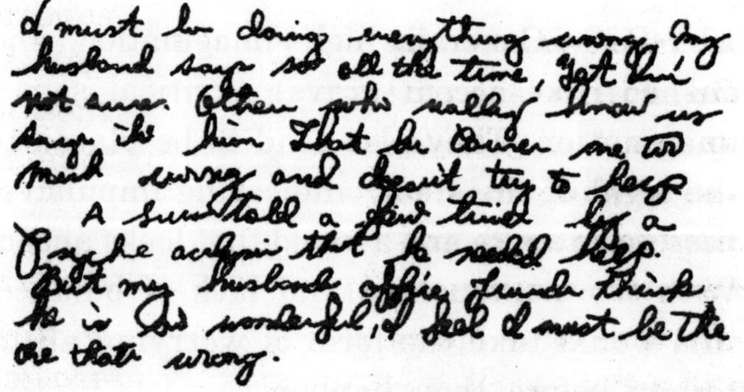

7. *Pressure*—Thick muddy : sensuality, strong passions, violence, vulgarity, untruthfulness, sometimes bad six habits or alcoholism.

7(a) *Uneven Pressure*—Instability, indecision, unequal will-power, unsustained energy, an eruptive, excitable, changeable temperament, impatience, nervousness and inclination to worry.

8. *Speed*—Quick but not fiuent : agitation, restless-ness, lack of discipline, impatience, impetuosity, tactlessness, aggressiveness possibly mental troubles.

9. *T-bars*—Varying from a heavy slash and the whiplash to a feeble touch, they show irresolution, and a fitful, defiant will.

10. *I-Dots*—Generally high : imagination, and dashed (like accent grave) : critical sense, imagination. They also tend to be placed to the right of the stem, indicating impulsiveness, impatience and a mind that looks ahead. With her nervousness and lack of balance, this would take the form of worrying about things before they happen.

11. *Punctuation*—Irregular, defective, neglected, agitation, stinginess, carelessness, impatience.

12. *Capitals*—Very tall (especially pronoun 'I'): pride, vanity, affectation, ceremoniousness, self-esteem, conceit, assertiveness, arrogance, a wish to be admired and love of luxury. The unattractive capitals show bad taste. Some are connected to the following letter, which suggests altruism, but since the writer's tendency is to connect all her letters, we

must find other signs to corroborate it. Throughout the letter, capitals are thrown in where they don't belong showing disorder, exaggeration.

13. *Beginning Strokes*—Ascending: contrariness, systematic opposition. Some initial strokes inturned : selfishness.

14. *Final Strokes Show Conflicing Traits*—The long, upflung terminals on some 'g's' and 'y's' together with u-shaped n's indicate beneficence, which would confirm the altruism of item 12. But we also find incurving terminals, especially on the pronoun 'I' indicating selfishness, egotism, acquisitiveness. However, the writer is not truly altruistic, since the base line and some of the letters are rounded, we can say that, while she is not truly goodhearted, she is capable of an occasional good-hearted gesture when it does not conflict with her own best interests.

15. *Upper Loops and Extension*—Inflated;

exaggeration, egotism, boastfulness, vanity.

16. Lower Loops Inflated—Physical vanity, pronounced sex-nature, materialism, love of money, avarice.

17. *Letter 'd' Made with Big Loop Swung to the Left*—A tendency to try to figure things out logically, even though she lacks the mentality for it and only confuses herself.

18. *Letter 'm' too Spread Out*—Bluff.

19. *Capital 'M'*—First stroke very high : pride self-interest, arrogance, ungainly proportions: exaggeration, lack of taste.

20. *Letter 'p'*—Shell-like hump : selfishness, positiveness, introversion.

21. *Capital 'P'* —In every single instance, the writer has capitalized 'P' where it begins a word, as she occasionally incorrectly capitalises other letters. We already have indicated disorder and exaggeration for this, but her preoccupation with P to such an

extreme degree and the fact that it plunges into the lower zone, undoubtedly symbolizes some obsession, probably sexual. The superfluous initial tick further points up abnormalcy.

Checking the list of dishonesty signs, we find:

1. Sinuous base line.
2. Some covering strokes.
3. Looped ovals.
4. Omitted letters.
5. Connecting strokes in wide shallow garlands.
6. Arcades (some pressed down to resemble garlands and combined with angularity).
7. Several o's opened to the left.
8. Retouched letters.
9. Jerky movement, complicated forms.
10. Lines tangled.

Since only four signs are needed to affirm dishonesty it is doubtedly affirmed The dominants in this handwriting are :

I. Mental and emotional instability with great nervous tension.

II. Pride, vanity, egotism and superficiality.

III. Bad taste, poor judgement.

IV. Dishonesty

V. Carelessness, lack of self-discipline.

VI. Sensuality, abnormal sex obsession.

Traits determined by a single symbol: Activity (mostly nervous since speed is jerky) sensuousness.

Other traits confirmed by repetition and/or by resultants:

restlessness	impatience
tendency to worry	confusion
needlessly	indecisiveness
irritability	complexity

spirit of contradiction
opposition
antagonism
fitful will (indomitable in defiance)
arrogance
exaggeration
bluff
affection
materialism
ambition
acquisitiveness
jealousy

moodiness
fickless
hypocrisy
disloyalty
untruthfulness
stinginess
selfishness
occasional goodheartedness

TO SUM UP

This unfortunate woman is a mental case, and cannot be judged by normal standards. Trying desperately to thing her way out of her troubles, she becomes more and more confused, exaggerating the difficulties she has, and imagining many she does not have.

Sexual preoccupations and frustrations are part of the sickness. Wanting desperately to be admired and desired, she defeats her wish by being haughty, selfish contrary antagonistic, impatient, lazy, slovenly and by pretending to be unresponsive. She automatically opposes everything and everyone. So great is her vanity, she believes she can attract love simply by her physical appeal.

She has no notion of order, no sense of proportion, no taste, no balance, no tact. When things do not go as she wants them to, she resorts to bluff, to outright lies and underhandedness, and is wholly untrustworthy. While she is not spontaneous or impulsive, she sometimes gives this impression because she deliberately indulges her whims unchecked by the least sense of what is appropriate and what is not, for she has neither judgement not instinct to help her, neither dignity not poise, and is so undisciplined that it appears she has had little training in this area.

Excitable, demanding, moody, changeable complex and contradictory, she can be secretive, inscrutable and inhibited one minute, impetuous, lively and talkative the next, confinding the most intimate and indiscreet details about herself to the first ready ear.

Selfish and stingy, she can surprise you with a goodhearted gesture, but she is most often obsessed with herself and her problems, to the extent she forgets and neglects important things.

Discord is her keynote. Because her superficial, false reasoning and conclusions have not achieved the results she desires, she is presently drowning in a sea of confusion, and badly needs professional help. If she does not get it, she may become violent and destructive.

* * * *

Of course, no experienced graphologist works as routinely and "by the book" as we have just done in the foregoing examples, intended only to demonstrate how a beginner may use this manual. The graphologist may be likened to the pianist who, taking in groups of notes at a glance, does not have to think in terms of each finger and each bit of technique he has learned, but is able swiftly and accurately to render the notes into music. What is essential, even for the beginner in graphology, is a good sense of observation, comprehension and a 'feeling' for the work. Skill comes with experience.

5

GRAPHO-THERAPEUTICS

(How to Improve Your Character and Personality Through Handwriting Exercise)

Grapho-therapeutics is the science pertaining to the therapy of the Graphic traits. Hand writing is oftenly called Brain writing because a circuit is established between brain and writing un-consciously.

Character sets the indivudual pattern of each handwriting and is inseparable from it, consequently, a voluntary handwriting change, once achieved, produces a corresponding change of character. How is this possible? The circuit established between brain and graphic gesture by the nervous system is two way. Thus the ability of the brain to influence the writing hand is reversible.

Proof of this fact is demonstrated by a very simple procedure most of us know from experience, namely, that the act of setting down in writing information, which we want to remember, or memorize, implants it in the mind as nothing else can.

The efficacy of graphotherapy was tested clinically at the Sorbenne between 1929 and 1931 by two eminent French scientists, Dr. Pleme Semet and Professor Charles Henry, Dealing principally, with alcoholics and with correcting bad habits in children, the experiement confirmed that the system intelligently and conscientiously applied, give positive results that are impressive.

In recent times Prof. Raymond Trillat has risen to the top of this field. Trillat uses some devices original with him, but he and all graphotherapists follow, in principle, the same plan the technique requires the subject to copy a handwriting exercise at least twice a day, morning and night, consciously modifying his script according to instructions applied by a competent psychographologist.

To understand graphotherapy, it is necessary to know a psychological princple, that a character flaw expresses itself exteriorly in bad habits, a characer quality in good habits. Laziness, for example, will cause the individual consistantly to be a late riser, to shirk work and all physical effort and to neglect duty. Conscientiousness will give as an indivudual who, even though handicapped by low nergy, will perform at all times the tasks expected of him. But the person who occasionally takes off to loaf cannot be judged lazy, any more than you can say that he who indulges once in a while in a splurge of spending is wasteful and extravagant. To be indicative of a flaw or a quality, the behavior must be frequent enough to be termed a habit.

Graphotherapy undertakes to break undesir-able habits which the hand follows as it writes, replacing them through repetitious exercise with desirable graphic habits. The hand, if you will, is retrained in specific writing gestures.

Handwriting exercises have much in common with the finger exercises employed in learning to play the piano. In the latter case, as long as the pianist must consciously think where to place each finger on the keyboard as he reads the music, he proceeds slowly and painfully, making errors. It is only after repetitious practice, when his fingers respond automatically and without conscious attention, that he can perform as an accom-plished artist. In graphotherapy, the goal is achieved when the desired handwriting change has passed the state of conscious application and imitation becoming automatic and normal to the hand.

The time required varies with the individual, because it is easier for some people than for others to break a habit. Another factor is how deeply entrenched the particular habit is, and whether it is a dominant or minor charactertistic. Average cases range from two to six months. The change can be facilitated by faithful application, but it can never be hurried. It takes patience, courage and the determination to continue as long as necessary to accomplish the aim.

Self Help Through Graphotherapy

While it unquestionably is beneficial and, in certain difficult cases, indispensible, there is no reason why someone with the intelligence to understand the principles of graphotherapy and to follow instructions should not use it to improve himself. There is no mystery about it, and anything which can be so enormously helpful should have the widest dissemination.

There is one point, however, where caution must be exercised—'and it is important'. "The elemental personality must always be respected". In doing the exercises, retain your natural tempo. If you are left-handed, continue to write that way, and write in your customary, individual script, making only the specific change, or changes, desired. Sometimes there is a tendency to revert to carefully made, childlike forms, this is to be avoided.

In the part "A Manual of Basic Graphology" of this book you will find in your own handwriting, the signs which reflect your flaws and shortcomings. You will also be able to determine how the signs should be modified. Remember the surest way to overcome a fault is to develop its positive opposite, otherwise you are merely suppressing it. For instance, if the problem it stinginess, you must strive to achieve generosity. One fights indolence and inertia by fortifying the will-power.

Next, choose a slogan from those offered at the end of this chapter or from any other available source.

Copy the chosen sentence in your characteristic handwriting. Note wherever the sign you wish to change occurs (it is helpful to mark the places in red pencil). Recopy the sentence, endeavouring, while otherwise writing normally, to make the change. Think about the graphic gesture necessary to achieve the change, and also think about what it is to accomplish for you.

Here are a few fundamental pointers to remember:

1. Assume a comfortable but correct writing posture with both feet on the floor, the spine straight (no slouching), left arm testing lightly on the writing surface, right arm free to move easily.

2. Use a pen which best suits your hand. The graphic habit you wish to break will offer enought resistance without having to cope with an unwieldy or bulky pen.

3. Establish a time, morning and night, to perform the exercise, and adhere to it. Writing is, of itself, an act of will. If you lack the energy, to do the exercise regularly of your own accord, you should solicit the help of someone who will see that you accomplish the task. Regularity and persistence are salient ingredients of the treatment.

4. Date each exercise, and keep all of them together so that you can check your progress.
5. At the outset, exaggerate the change you are trying to achieve, but as it comes easier to your hand, cease to emphasize it an aim for naturalness.
6. If several changes are desired, accomplish only one at a time, unless they are interrelated.
7. A graphotherapist closely checks a patient's exercise to keep him on the right track where self-therapy is practiced, you must examine your own work constantly, noting where you have succeeded, where you have failed. don't be discouraged if it is difficult. Remember that the hand is obeying the negative characteristic with which you are grappling. Concentrate with greater determination on making it obey you. You will never win a more satisfying victory.
8. Sometimes a bad habit, driven out will return. If this occurs, you will find yourself backsliding into the defective

graphism you eradicated. Resume your exercises at once.

THE EXERCISES SLOGAN

While a meaningful slogan is not essential to graphotherapy which operates effectively using only the mechanism of the writing hand in repetitious exercise, it is logical to avail oneself of an assist from applied autosuggestion, that is, a suggestion made by the conscious intelligence to the subconscious intelligence. Applied autosuggestion and graphotherapy relate very naturally, since each employs a type of conscious repetition which achieves a desired end through the intricate workings of the mind.

For this reason, an exercise with a positive message speficially tailored to the individual's problem. Thus for a timid subject, Seneca's encouraging thought is prescribed : "It is not because things are difficult that we don't dare; it is because we don't dare that things are difficult".

Some people are easily wearied by repetition, if this leads to carelessness, change to a new sentence to get back on the toes.

It will be no problem to choose an appropriate slogan for yourself. Readings are the following list, you will find your mind fastening on one or another, with a sense of its rightness for you.

SAMPLE EXERCISES

1. It is not because things are difficult that we don't dare; it is because we don't dare that things are difficult.

2. Life is a battle in which you are to share your pluck. Despair and postponement are cowardice and defeat. Man was born to succeed not to fail—Thoreau.

3. The will to accomplish all that it want to do is mine to draw upon. I have the energy to make quick decisions and to act when action is called for; and I have the strength to resist what is unworthy nor unwise.

4. Lord, give me the serenity to accept that which I cannot change; the courage to change what can be changed and the wisdom to discern the one from the other.

   —*Alcoholics Anonymous*

5. A personal problem, seen in its relative importance to the universe, to its magnitude, its order and its beauty, is a small and fugitive thing. As part of that universe, I can and I will support mine, knowing that this, too shall pass.

6. I live in the present, calmly, peaceably, courageously, confident in the knowledge that a goal is reached one step at a time, and that when the future becomes the present, it will come bearing the sweet fruits of all the positive thoughts and efforts which I put into today.

7. I resolve to have will-power, to develop my selfhood, to make quick decisions, trusting my judgement, to accomplish all the worth-while things. I want to do, and to cultivate the gifts and God has given me.

8. To be bound to any vice is to be a slave I was born free, and I want, I can and I dare to reject any and every enslaving habit being always master of myself.

9. The soul is great, ardent vast. Confined,

it lives in torment. And so, I open my heart and my mind to give it infinite space to communicate with all around my thereby enriching my knowledge and my experience.

10. I am filled with the spirit of gladness. I have a sense of freedom and enjoyment. I am filled with an expectancy of good things. The energy of life flows through me.

* * * *

Raymond Trillat says, "If you can study someone's handwriting and deduce ideas about his character; why can't you reverse the process? By modifying his handwriting, perhaps you can modify his personality".

An associate of the Psycho-Pedagogic Centre of the University of Paris. Trillat has since won the support of doctors, teachers and psychologists for his success in clearing up mental disturbances in children by changing their handwriting whether it is told to a pupil to keep on making long strings of *eeeeeee* or to concentrate on such rounded letters as a, b, and g. It alwasy has its reasons.

When he first began his experiements with children. Trillat found that many of their inner problems showed up clearly in their writing. The introverts had difficulty connecting their letters; the timid tended to squeeze all theirs together. Gradually, Trillat concerted a set of corrective exercises designed to give children a sense of "continuity, creation and equilibrium". In overcoming a defect, in any of these elements, a child must first develop a feeling of rhythm, melody and harmony.

Trillat found that many neurotic children, some of them stutterers could not follow through 'They were children who couldn't even open a door with a single gesture. They would pull it in a series of hesitant, jerky movements". Such cases start out with a series of connected, then has them move on to variations . For the particularly nervous be designed special "Sedative exercises" and for the unstable, a series of plaits to develop "continuity" in a discontinued movement. "Those who squeeze their letters practice broad, sweeping motions and those who spread their letters two much through lack of a sense of harmony

Later each child is encouraged to find his own creative personality by forming his letters individually and to develop equilibrium by slanting his writing in one direction and making his letters all one size.

All too often, emotional problems leads to illegibility, and illegibility leads to more emotional problems like remedial reading graphotherapy does not change the basic personality, it is merely one way to break down certain kinds of emotional barriers. It frees children from the restrictions imposed by the fact of having to write and contributing to emancipating them from deeper problems and help their personalities to blossom.

6

MEDICAL GRAPHOLOGY

Medical Graphology is a very important part of this science which can benefit an individual in number of ways. It can also be used as prophylactic as well as curative. Disease manifest much before in the form of graphotrait then they actually happen, any proper curative preventive step taken at that stage will help in coming that diseases effectively.

The act of writing is, in part, physiological movement involving brain, nervous system, muscles and supporting vital organs. Since physical disorders, of whatever nature, affect the whole system, weakening it, changing posture or attitude, breaking normal rhythm and thereby influencing physiological movment, if follows that these disorders produced visible phenomena in handwriting. Modern graphology has interpreted many of these pathological and psychopathological graphisms.

Until recent years, research was badly handicapped by doctors' and hosptials' unwillingness to cooperate, but with skepticism gradually breaking down in these quarters, we can expect faster progress and perhaps some more startling discoveries like that of Alfred Kanfer on cancer (as described in our Introduction), or the graphometric findings on epilepsy by Gobineau and Perron.

Following are some of the disorders for which definite graphic signs have been found.

A

Glandular troubles invariably produce twisted upper loops in handwriting.

Fig. 1 was written by a woman with a thyroid deficiency.

life which God
days be bright

Fig. 2 shows how puberty has twisted the handwriting of an eleven-year-old girl.

the tree is

Fig. 3 is a fourteen year-old boy in full puberty. There is twisting not only in the upper loops not throughout.

Fig. 4 is an example of a woman in the menopause.

Fig. 5 shows the violent twisting in the script of a sexually impotent man of fifty-five.

Twisted handwriting may occur at any age, and may result from emotional as well as from physical English.

B

Cardic disorders cause sudden jerks of the hand as it writes, which correspond to intermissions in the heartbeat. This shows up abrupt breaks in pen stroke.

you know if Robert

C

Respiratory ailments produce the same unexpected interruptions in strokes, but they are usually less accentuated and are accompanied by dots left where the pen rested on the paper, as if the scriptor having trouble to breathe and write at the same time, has paused to take a breath.

D

Locometer Ataxia is a disease of spinal cord with involuntary movement, which patient cannot coordinate. Handwriting generally is jerky and smeary in appearance, with strokes that are short, pointed, heavy, muddy and unequal in height. Words descend, finals are incompleted and there are useless little signs in the middle of letters.

E

Kidney disorders cause the sufferer to favour the side in pain.

Note the curious cure of M in the above specimen which reflects the bending of the body at the waist.

F

Live trouble appears is slow, heavy curled up writing.

G

Alcoholism always causes handwriting to descend. The alcoholic's script may also have a smeary appearance, or look shaky due to rembling, and sometimes there will be violent pen strokes T-crosses will be weak or inconsistent.

might call them.
"Nervousness caused
by alcohol" thanks.
am a salesman for
52 L.D. [illegible]

H

Neurasthenia, melancholia, sadness and deep depression—are portrayed in a decayed script, with letters badly formed, hesitations, frequent erasures or scratch outs, useless punctuation muddiness, signs of trembling and lines that plunge downward.

I

In extreme cases of **depression** where the subject approaches 'suicide' it shows very clearly in the handwriting principally in the signature.

Pulver's description is a cross under the line, formed by a prolongation of the capital terminal and the final which cuts sharply to the left. From objective experience, any two lines which cross beneath the signature indicate a suicidal tendency.

Other signs as showing 'an intention of suicide' are letters that jump out of line signatures of the left a barring of initial capitals.

Nervous surexcitation gives a jerky effect and a wavering base line. The script is erratically variable with pressure, speed and size altering suddenly.

J

Hysteria creates irregularity, big pen movements, exageration of certain small letters strange forms, heavy pressure, ink-filled upper loops and frequent fistform strokes (heavy in the middle, tapering art ends.)

K

Bad Sex Habits. Handwriting shows lack of self assurance, of self-reliance and of strength. Capitals are contracted, strokes hesitant, heavy and trembling, i-dots are very low and usually to the left.

INVERSION (homo-sexuality)

Sexual inverts generally are:

1. Completely introverted (ovals closed, looped and double looped)

2. Sensuous and Epicurean (heavy pressure, loops inkfilled, long lower loops).
3. Capricious (long plunging cross on x).

Inversion also appears in various strokes that are turned counter to normal; or in some unlikely stroke like a little flag of the D.

M

INSANITY takes a number of different forms, and its symbols are many and diverse. Any generalization, therefore, will short of covering the question. An attempt to establish definite symbols must immediately cope with the fact that, whereas physical disabilities lend themseleves to statistical measurement (as by the graphometic system), the mind, which is so clusive that it can be neither defined exactly not located in the body, is too multifarious in its kinds and degrees of aberration to be readily categorized.

This should not deter graphologists from seeking specific answers. We already have a few which aid in the diagnosis and treatment of mental derangement.

There has been conjecture that some mental disorder may have physiological causes or contributing factors. Certainty, it has been noted that the mentally disturbed often have the twisted upper loops which indicate glandular troubles.

It must be remembered that no single signs standing alone, ever is sufficient to prove mental abnormalcy. However, certain precursory signs warn the graphologists when a mental disturbance is brewing. They are:

1. Small s & r large than other middle zone letters (sign of exaltation)

2. Ascending final of small d ends in a complex convolution.
3. Capitals frequently used where they do not belong.

4. Frequent underscoring.
5. Bizarre ornamentation.
6. Marks superimposed over letters (concealing strokes)

7. Agitated handwriting with exaggeratedly high capitals and big pen movements.

Some forms of insanity are more recognizable than others, and the handwriting will reflect the same confusion which exists in the demented mind. In addition to the signs listed above, lines may be tangled, there will be ink spots, frequent scratch outs and marks overs, unnecessary punctuation, unintelligible heiroglyphies, twisting, a combination of arcades and angular forms, and frequent omissions (or duplications) of letters and words.

N

PARANOIA is one form of mental aberration which is not always apparent. The individual may seem "different" or "strange", but unless the condition becomes acute, it can go undetected. Nevertheless (as established by Dr. Genil Perrin), it is possible to find paranoia in handwriting.

It has four characteristics, shown below, and all four must be present simultaneously. At least one of the symbols listed under each of the four categories must be distinct in the handwriting or supported by other signs in the same categories in order to classify it as paranoiac.

1. Inflated Ego

Superelevated, flourished capitals (paticularly L & I) t-bars long heavy, ascending and ending in dubs.

2. Lack of Social Adaptabitity

Angular forms
broken connections which, if carried through would be garlands
fast speed
heavy pressure
long, high t-bars with hooks
acutely angular t-dots.

3. False Judgement

high pointed t-bars
pointed terminals
i-dots high and dashed
wide margins
inflated upper and lower extensions
tangling uneven motor sequence
handwriting irregular and angular.

4. Mistrustfulness and Apprehension

terminals long, heavy, sharp and downflung t-bars long, heavy, sharp and down-flung
heavy pressure
ovals closed
periods replaced by dashes
unnecessary initial strokes
upper and lower extensions long and with breaks down strokes firm and straight.

Dear Friend – You will be
hearing more of me soon in
"Let's Make Love" Marilyn

Specimen was written by the late unfortunate **Marily Monroe**, and shows all the characteristics of paranoia.

1. Inflated ego appears in the superelevated, flourished capitals, especially the L which seems to stand on a piedestal.

2. Lack of social adaptability is revealed in certain angular forms, such as the base of b in be and the triangle in s of soon. It is further confirmed by heavy pressure and broken garland connections (le-ts).

3. False judgement is betrayed in the pointed terminals and the tangled if of you.

4. Mistrustfulness and apprehension are in the long, heavy sharp, and down flung terminals, heavy pressure, closed ovals, unnecessary initial strokes (of the Ms), breaks in long upper extensions (l of Marilyn), most down strokes firm and straight.

O

SCHIZOPHRENIA (Split personality) is characterized by conflicting ideas and a break with the world of reality. As with other forms of mental illness, graphic symbols differ because there are varying kinds and degree of conflict. For instance one type may want to make friends but it anti-social in behavior, or completely unable to follow accepted social usage, thus defeating the desire. This type often stands off, critical and aloof, wondering why people don't make friendly overtures to him and seething with a sense of rejection Another, mentally dull, may simulate intellectual interests and set goals completely beyond his reach.

The definition of 'schizoid' is a dislocated personality. The individual unable to deal with the stresses of life, retreats into a distorted world of his own making. Graphically, schizophrenia is translated into abnormal strokes, accentric pressure, grotesque froms, changing slant, bizzare, scrolls, triangles or circles, too wide spacing between words, varying motor sequence, irregular base line, words tapering off, extravagant pen movements, letters split apart, automatism.

Occasionally, people show a combination of paranoias and schizophrenia conditions. This is true of the following specimen.

It reads, "In this room are tables and chairs". While it has all four paranoiac characteristics, the peculiar combination of illegible lightness (loss of contact with the word).

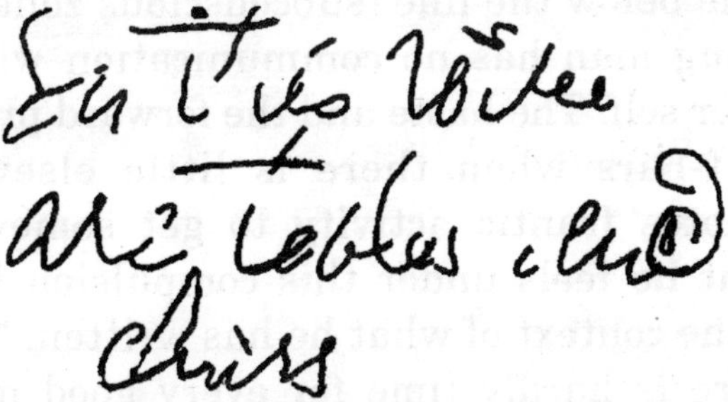

With abnormal pressure on t-bars i-dots and upflung terminal of and, the purposeless pen movement, jumpy base line (disorientation) and changing slant (instability), together with completely split apart letters (like the h in this) suggests the dislocated personality of the schizoid.

The followng specimens reflect the variety of symbols in schizophrenia due to differences in the nature of the aberrations. Only the result (the break with reality) puts them in the same classification.

Much of Fig. 21 is illegible, due to a radical departure from accepted forms (inability to follow good social custom). The pen movement is extravagant and erratic, i is omitted from aid, but the stern of a dotted. With all the activity in the upper zone and very little below the line (subconscious zone), this young man has no communication with his inner self. The haste and the forward pressure on t-bars when there is little elsewhere, denotes frantic activity to get somewhere. That he feels under this compulsion is also in the context of what he has written. "Today there is hardly time for every good man to aid his country" this is a typical schizoid conflict, in that while he strives for recognition, he feels superior (excessive height of letters) to those by whom he would be recognized. In the last word the o has almost dropped out of sight, u begins above the middle zone (an extraordinary split between those two letters, n looks like i.e., and t is written over it. This writing-over is done several times, and shows his disorientation.

The slant of inhuman handwriting in Fig. 22 (which gives one a sense of vestigo) bespeak withdrawal, coldness and concientiousness. The lance like t-cross (in country) shows real wickedness. At the sametime, the pronounced arcades say that the individual seeks to attract attention and admiration making a schizoid conflict. A sign of abnormately is the presence of mixed angles with arcades another is the automatism. Note, too, how the lower extension of f in the first line turns left instead of right, making a sharp angle, the shark toothed appearance of eir (their last line), the angular connection in aid showing variation in size between a &

d. Rigidity and heavy pressures combined with the backward slant, shows meanness and resistance, and the compressed e's tell that she is narrowminded and susceptible. Her ardor being of a negative type she would likely become heated only in defence of her narrow views or in opposition to others.

Now is the time for
good men to come to
aid of the country

Above, we have another backhand specimen with a completely different appearance. Slant, the closed, looped ovals and the returned stroke on the letter I, show pronounced introversion, the balloned loops indicate egocentrism to an abnormal degree. The descending, heavy t-bars express resistance and a tendency to destructiveness. The l is omitted from mailed. All this, together, with tangling (confusion) erratic pressure and surexcitation, make her a dangerous individual with an imagination that completely distorts reality.

7

CONCLUSION

After many ups and downs, characterized by intense persistence among many dedicated psychologists, graphology is currently enjoying a long overdue and richly deserved renaissance as a fully recognized and respected scientific discipline.

Modern dynamic psychology and psychiatry, in comparatively recent years, have made great strides in laying bare the basic nature of our mental and nervous process, both normal and abnormal Psychoanalysis has illuminated the vast worlds of the unconscious and the subconscious. Like the newer characterology, they have advanced and will continue to advance graphology, the original goal of which was simply to analyze a person's character through his or her handwriting.

Now both graphology and graphotherapy show us how to improve that character by analysis and synthesis. Advancing side by side with other modern discoveries in mental science and personality research graphotherapy is well on its way to establish new bases, theories and methods.

Now with the help of this book you can easily decide its efficacy for yourself by putting it to the test.

8

DICTIONARY OF CHARACTER TRAITS AND THEIR GRAPHOLOGICAL SYMBOLS

Absent-Mindedness

Omitted 't-bar'; omitted i-dot; p without hump.

Acquisitiveness (Avarice) (Greed)

Words crowded; initial books; finals short or retrogressive; no margins; inflated lower loops; 'm' humps' like ovals or half-ovals; 'M' curling initial and final strokes.

Activity (Mental)

Ascending lines; superior connected; very quick and simplified; rhythmic and firm; t-bars post-placed; i-dot an-accent; i-dot joned to following letter; tall upper loops; 'p' tong like; 'p' lower ext. curved right; 'p' simplified, signature final a zigzag.

Activity (Physical and sportive)

Large with great movement; angular, heavy pressure, down strokes firm; rapid; long lower loops; abrupt final on M; signature a zigzag.

Adaptability (Flexibility)

Round or curved; garland connections; evenpressure; rapid; capitals moderate.

Aesthetic Interests (Artistic taste, culture).

Graceful curves; all letters harmoniously proportioned; artistic original forms; well spaced; artistic arrangment; wide margins all four sides; capital pointed; g like figure 8; L with descending, curved final; 'p' tong like; ascending final on 'p'. 'P' nicely curved, graceful and simple; 'P' set on a base.

Affectation (Artificiality)

Inferior garlands; big arcades; ornate and artificial; excessively large capitals; too much space between words and lines; triangular lower loops; 'm' with looped base; flourished initial strokes on 'M'; 'p' tall upper extension; P set on a base.

Affection (Sentiment)

Inclined, curved; superior garlands; looped base on 'm'.

Aggressiveness

Angular; heavy; hasty; t-bars thin and long or ascending and thick at end; accentuated horizontal finals; lower loopsreplced by return stroke to right; signature final first left, then right; signature final plunging either left or right.

Agitation

Constantly changing slant; hesitant, jerky connections; tangled and confused; uneven margins; uneven pressure; hasty; irregular punctuation.

Alcoholism

Descending base lines, shaky connections thick and muddy.

Alltruism (Beneficence)

Large; round; widely spaced; legible; capitals joined to following letters; ascending finals; return stroke of 'y' and 'g' ascending above middle zone; very round 'm', 'v' final covering what follows.

Ambition

Ascending base line, arcades; form even pressure; rapid; ascending t-bars; large capitals; long upper and lower extensions, 'M' middle hump highest (social ambition); ascending signature; signature under scored by final of first letter.

Amiability (Friendliness)

Inclined soft, round; garland connections; garland 'm', superior garlands.

Anger

Rigidly angular; heavy slashing strokes t-bars and finals long and pointed like swords; letters tormented and ungraceful; heavy, irregular underscoring.

Apprehensiveness

Upper and lower extensions broken.

Ardor (Zealousness)

Inclined; ascending base line; left margin widening as it descends; heavy; ascending t-bars; 'd' has loop ending with horizontal right turned stroke; if this horizontal stroke turns left, ardor is curbed by the will.

Arrogance

Large capitals; very tall capitals; first stroke of 'M' very high.

Assertiveness

Wide open orals; heavy; 't-bars' slung down; very tall capitals; finals abrupt and dub-shaped.

Audacity (Boldness)

Very large or large : wide connecting strokes, clongated dub-shaped finals.

Calmness

Even pressure; slow speed; t-bars normal pressure; evenly spaced; i-dots round and justy placed; no long terminals, no great movements of pen.

Carefulness (Prudence, Accuracy, Precision)

Modium size; superior connected; ovals closed; regular form, even spacing; great legibility; even margins; even pressure; t-bars normal pressure, evenly spaced on stem; i-dots round and justly spaced; firm conventional punctuation; capitals figure shaped; abrupt final on M; 'p' tong-like; signature protected by dashes; envelopes very legibly addressed.

Carelessness (Disorder, Neglectfulness)

Irregular form, spacing bad; words and

lines tangled; illegible, uneven margins; t-bars and i-dots omitted; misplaced punctuation; capitals used where they do not belong; 'p' a single stroke without a hump; envelopes illegibly addressed.

Cautiousness

Vertical, all ovals closed; t-bars and i-dots light and pre-placed; punctuation accentuated; no exaggerated movement of the pen.

Ceremoniousness (Formality)

Very large; arcades; flourishes; large capitals; triangular, lower extensions.

Clarity of Ideas (clearmindedness)

Connected; fluent, good spacing between words and lines; legible; even pressure.

Coarseness (crudeness)

Inferior, illegible; thick, muddy writing; ink-filled lower loops; ungraceful forms, ugly, dub-shaped finals.

Cold-Heartedness

Very reclined; rigid and angular; possibly heavy; abrupt finals. Descending finals, heavy and printed

Complexity

Ovals looped, words and lines tangled.

Conceit (Variety)

Inflated; very tall capitals; inferior arcades; ornate and artificial forms; looped beginning strokes; balloned upper and lower loops; triangular lower loops, all flourishes, 'd' ending in scroll; 'D' stretched wide; 'M' humpse wide apart, heads depressed.

Concentration

Small; i-dots round and justly placed.

Confusion

Words and lines tangled; inferior illegible.

Conscientiousness

Level base line; ovals completely open; perfectly legible, i-dots round and justly placed above stem.

Contrains

Ascending initial strokes; 'S' a nearby straight stroke.

Conventionality (Mediocrity, Confirmity, Routineness; Banality)

Inferior lightly inclined; medium size; inferior connected; arcades; exaggeratedly regular form; ornate and artifical forms, legible as printing; margins rigidly even; careful punctuation; copybook beginning strokes; 'M' middle stroke plunging downward.

Courage

Concave base line; large; wide spacing, heavy firm pressure; long, strong t-bars and strokes; accentuated horizontal finals; lower extension of 'p' curved right, 'P' hump detached.

Critical Mind

Pointed above curved base line; i-dots a reversed accent; signature final claw-shaped.

Cruelty (Harshness)

Angular; long, very heavy t-bars, heavy descending t-bars; long printed t-bars; i-dots like short arrow; dub shaped ascending or descending finals or pointed finals; final a large loop ending with sharp point; signature final claw-shaped.

Deceitfulness

Sinuous base line, inferior garlands; looped ovals. ambiguous illegible forms.

Defiance (Rebelliousness)

Ovals open on left-side, final of 'v' rears up and separates itself form rest of word.

Depression (Discouragement)

Descending base line; left margin narrowing as it descends; low t-bars, descending signatures.

Despondency

Plunging base line; light 't-bars; long and excessively heavy, descending; above the stem and covering other letters; hooked; Determination (Firmness, Resoluteness, Rigidity)

Angular; heavy; rapid; long heavy t-bars; hooked t-bars; whiplash like t-bars; short; dub-shaped finals.

Directness

Natural and simplified; rapid; t-bars post-placed; no initial strokes; short terminals.

Dominativeness

T-bars too long and heavy; t-bars long, heavy and above the stem; t-bars hooked; 'd' tall upswept ending looped high 'P' a curlicue atop a stick; 'v' final covers what follows (sign g protectiveness and domination).

Eccentricity

Bizzare, grotesque forms; unnecessary loops, scrolls, circles etc., vary t-bars; illegible signature.

Economy-Minded (Frugality, Stringiness)

Crowded; left margin narrowing as it descends; narrow or no margins; poor punctuation; short finals; 'm' strokes broken.

Efficiency

Pointed above curved base line; regular form; natural simplified and quick; fluent form; rapid; t-bars replaced by continuing upstroke, no beginning strokes; short or no finals.

Egotism

Very reclined; large flourished capitals; hooked finals; looped finals; large, heavy convolutions on finals; inflated under loops; L-base loop enlarged; M fist stroke highest; M with hooks; M final prolonged to underscore what follows all regressive strokes to the left; signature under and overscored.

Emotional Nature

Inclined or very inclined; connecting strokes unequal.

Energy

Ascending; large with great movements of the pen; angular; rapid long, strong t-bars, often exaggerated; abuse of punctuation; abrupt final on M cadenced, firm and progressive, energetic handwriting appears to stand out from the page as if 'en relief'.

Enthusiasm

Ascending base line; characterized by long, high, heavy strokes, enthusiasm can be measured by the length of t-bars, the unreasonable amount of (or pressure on) exclamation marks, letters that grow larger at the end of the word; elongated commas; excessive period; P with large, balloned loop.

Exaggeration (Extravagance)

Very large; flourished; too widely spaced; wide right margin; widening left margin; capitals used where they do not belong; upper loops inflated, ungainly proportion M.

Exitability

Constently changing slant; base line

varying; words and lines tangled; t-bars high above stem, uneven.

Expansiveness

Large; excessively open.

Extraversion

Very large; large; open ovals; superior legible.

Fastidiousness

Small; wide right margin; slow.

Fickleness (Capriciousness, Inconstancy)

Varying slant, varying or vary or convex base-line; inferior glands; varying pressures; concave t-bars.

Frankness

Open ovals, rapid and spontaneous.

Generosity

Large, curved widely spaced, ascending finals; rounded 'm'.

Gentleness

Round; light 'M' in garlands.

Goodheartedness

Round; 'm' rounded; 'M' in garlands with very rounded base.

Gourmet

Handwriting is generally slow, effeminate soft spindle shaped.

Harmoniousness

Superior rounded; even, well proportioned margins; P nicely curved, raceful and simple.

Honesty

Harmonious; firm base line; ovals open; simple and natural; clear and legible; spontaneous; strong t-bars; signature easy to read.

Humor

Wary t-bars; crack-the-whip t-bars; crescent shaped I-dots; signature with wary or curved underscore.

Hypocrisy (Insincerity)

Inferior reclined; inferior garlands, ovals open at bottom; ovals closed and looped.

Idealism

Very clean and generally light; i-dots very high and light; ascending final; ball upper extensions; 'd' ending in upswept vertical stroke; P a hat very high above stem.

Imagination

Large; superior disconnected; unusual connections; artistic original forms; superior illegible; t-bars above stem; i-dots round and high, i-dots like accents; very large question mark; upper extensions tall; 'd' has loop ending with horizontal right turned stoke or left turned stroke (for curbed imagination) 'd' with balloon terminal; 'p' upper loop very high; P with large ballooned loop; P made in single stroke; s smaller than the other middle zone letters; fluent figures.

Imagination (Bizzare or Abnormal Type)

Words and lines very tangled; P a stem topped by strange 'hat' with hooks; v spread out.

Impatience

Wide connecting strokes; superior illegible; uneven pressure; hasty; excessively long thin t-bars; short or long painted finals; 'p' a simple stroke without a hump; S like comma.

Inactivity (Energy, low)

Varying slant; possible disconnected; round and soft; garlands; light uneven pressure; slow; uneven spacing; preplaced t-bars and I-dots.

Indecisiveness (Hesitation)

Reclined; varying slant; varying base line; soft very small; hesitant or jerky connections; inferior illegible; uneven pressure; very slow and hesitant; weak t-bars; preplaced t-bars; concave t-bars; preplaced t-bars; concave t-bars; preplaced i-dots; useless; exaggerated punctuation; pending in loop left of first stroke.

Independence (Some non-confirmity)

Very reclined or vertical, tall capitals; angular; widely spaced; superior illegible; finals descending beneath line or short or dub-shaped, first stroke on M, N, W high, movement that goes contrary to conventional direction; signature underscored by final of last letter.

Indifference (detachment)

Very reclined or vertical.

Ingenuousness (Naivete)

Excessively rounded and soft ovals; too open; inferior legible.

Initiative

Ascending base line; large heavy; rapid; accentuated horizontal finals; P ending in loop right of stem.

Instability

Varying or sinuous base line; slant; speed; pressure and margins erratic and variable; wide connected strokes, exaggerated irregular form; weak or concave t-bars; too frequent under-scoring.

Intelligence

Superior (harmonius) small; either disconnected or connected; superior garlands; natural simplified and quick; fluent; artistic and original; nicely spaced; superior legible; superior light; even pressure; very quick and simplified; post-placed i-dots; i-dots a sharp accent; well proportioned capitals; tall upper extensions; lower loop turned left instead of right for fluency; 'g' made like figure 8; I a simple stick; M amplified; M with all lumps even, m simply made; simplified p P two curved; simple movements; P implified and swift; signature very large, but no flourishes or scorings; no variation between signature and text; wary vertical paragraph.

Intuition

Superior disconnected; generally curved; pressure light with shading stick like I.

Introversion (Inhibition, Tension)

Reclined; very small; sharp narrow connection ovals closed; inferior illegible convex t-bars; compressed upper loops; 'p' with shell like hump; signature left of centre.

Irritability

Angular words and lines tangled; heavy pressure or uneven; t-bars too long and heavy; dub-shaped t-bars or i-dots; short pointed finals.

Jealousy

Very or acutely inclined; heavy or uneven pressure. High-flying t-bars; t-stem final incurved to make the cross; i-dots like accents large; inflated capitals; incurving hooks; tall upper extensions; a signature overscored.

Judgement (Good)

Superior connected; connecting strokes equal; pointed above curved base line.

Judgement (Poor)

Varying slant, inferior disconnected or inferior connected, words and lines tangled.

Kindness

Inclined; curved; ascending finals simple and clear; free of any pointed strokes; M in garlands with pronouncedly round base.

Logic

Superior connected; legible; even pressure; d-stem a big, left-slung loop.

Loyalty

Harmonious; open ovals. signature very legible.

Luxury (Love of)

Very large; too widely spaced; wide right margin; left margin widening as it descends; heavy supper-elavated capitals.

Materialism

Inferior connected; heavy; muddy i-dots; inflated lower loops; no loop on top in; m lumps made like ovals or half ovals; M middle stroke plunging downward; figures referring to money better traced than others.

Mathematical Aptitude

Usually small; capitals figure-shaped; figures simplified; clear and lightly square; figures well and quickly traced.

Melancholy

Descending or concave baseline a characteristics; irregular.

Memory

All ovals very round and well traced regular form; i-dots round and justly placed.

Mendaciousness (Untruthfulness)

Sinews base line.

Moderation

Medium size; short upper extensions; no variation between signature and text.

Modesty (Simplicity)

Capitals slightly higher than small letters; handwriting simple and plain; capitals printed; P simplified and swift; signature moderate sized and unflourished.

Nervousness

Constantly changing slant; shaky; jerky or uneven connections; size altering suddenly; exaggeratedly irregular forms; illegibility sharp strokes with frequent retouches; left margin widening as it descends; pressure spasmodic; strokes broked of m.

Non-Confirmity

Changing slant; large; angular; superior illegible; large; twisted capitals, paragraphy descending vertically.

Obstinacy (Stubbornness)

Very reclined or vertical; angular; heavy; t-bars descending with heavy pressure; t-bars down curved; t-bars hooked; whiplash t-bar; L terminating to left; p lower extension a left-turned hook; final of S left-turned.

Optimism

Base line ascending; left margin widening as it descends; t-bars ascending; ascending signature.

Orderliness

Connecting strokes even length; regular form; nicely disposed arrangement; even margins; i-dots round and justly placed; perfect punctuation; L resembling 4 figure.

Originality (Inventiveness)

Superior disconnected; superior arcades; original and individual forms and connections; i-dots a sharp accent; printed capitals, P two curved; simple strokes; P one simple stroke; V spread out; signature paragraph in superior writing.

Patience

Curved with light pressure; very slow t-bars.

Perseverance (Persistency)

Level; concave base line; superior connected; angular; firm even pressure; excessively long t-bars; accentuated horizontal finals.

Pessimism

Descending base line; useless exaggerated punctuation; phrases or sentences formed by dashes; d left turned and ending below base line.

Pleasure (Love of)

Love lower loops;

Practicality

Inferior connected; narrow or no margins; short or no finals; short upper extensions; long lower loops; no top loop on L.

Prejudice

Angular, M final crossing back and left.

Pride

Large or very small; tall; very tall and inflated capitals; too wide left margin; looped beginning strokes; base loop on L upflung; initial stroke highest on M; 3 hump instead of 2 on M; upper loop on p very high; P made with a curlicue stop a stick; P exaggeratedly tall; signature larger than text; signature capitals over-sized and inflated; signature underscored.

Procrastination

Handwriting very slow; soft and inconsistent, t-bars and i-dots preplaced.

Pugnacity (Combativeness)

Reclined; heavy; hasty; t-bars descending and heavy t-bars descending and heavy; t-bars and finals excessively heavy, i-dots heavy and accent-shaped; ascending dub shaped finals; pointed finals; M abrupt final; signature final plunging right.

Reasonableness

Medium size; carfully connected; nicely spaced; legible; even pressure; precise punctuation; moderation in everything.

Refinement (Delivery)

Small; light; i-dots very high and light.

Reserve (Restraint, uncommunicativeness)

Reclined or vertical. medium size;

connections narrow; ovals closed or looped; wide left or right margin; very short t-bars but superior script; modest size capitals; L terminating left; no loop at top of L; initial stroke on M a closed loop; lower extension of p curved left; final of P crossing left; signature under and overscored; paragraph encircling signature.

Very reclined; angular; heavy and firm; descending; heavy t-bars; t-bars strongly hooked.

Responsiveness

Very inclined; garland connections; fluent meter sequence.

Secretiveness

Very reclined; ovals closed, looped, and double looped; inferior illegible; L terminating to left; M final crossing back and left; M lumps wide apart, heads depressed; signature illegible; signature protected by dashes.

Self-Confidence

Signature very large but unflourished; signature moderated sized and unflourished; signature underscored.

Self-Control (Self-Discipline)

Vertical; level base line; letters even; well spaced; legible; firm; even; calm strokes.

Selfishness

Very reclined; angular; capitals beginning and/or ending with hooks initial strokes inturned; final on upturned hook; final a large loop ending with shap point; final a large, heavy convolution; initial stroke on M a hook; M final prolonged to underscore what follows, p with shell like hump; signature overscored; signature final circling over and enclosing name; envelope illegible addressed.

Self-Protectiveness

Signature overscored; signature final circling over and enclosing name.

Self-Satisfaction

Very tall capitals; base loop upflung on L; signature underscored by finals of first letter.

Sensitivity (Sensibility)

Inclined; superior disconnected; superior irregular form; light; star shaped t; d with looped stem; stick like I; amplified m; M made like enlarged m.

Sensuousness (Passion)

Very inclined or acutely inclined; illegible; heavy; loops ink-filled generally muddy appearance; muddy i-dots; finals descending and dub-shaped; lower loops inflated.

Sincerity

Inclined; firm base line; all ovals open; spontaneousness and natural; legible.

Snobbism (Pretension)

Ornate and artificial forms; too wide left margin; triangular lower loops; M initial stroke very large or flourished; p lower extension ending in left-tunred hook; P flourished and unharmonious; P a stem with strange 'hat' and hooks; P exaggeratedly tall.

Sociability

Round; arcades; superior legible, narrow or no margins.

Spirituality

Superior light; high; light i-dot; ascending finals; tall upper extensions; ascending d-stem.

Sponteneity

Rapid; very quick and simplified; D

Ending in upswept right curve or in loop and right turned stroke; p lower extension curved right.

Stability (Balance, Contancy, Poise)

Vertical or superior lightly inclined; level base line; connecting strokes equal, well spaced; even margin; even pressure; firm t-bars that cross stem evenly; i-dots round and justly placed; capitals slightly higher than small letters; M with all humps relatively even.

Stupidity

Unharmonious; slow; banal; vulgar; graceless; ornate forms.

Submissiveness (Humility, Obedience, Passivity, Resignation, Timidity)

Small capitals; excessively round; light; monotonous and slow t-bars too short; descending light t-bars; t-bars low on stem; i-dots very light; capitals no higher than small letters; upper extensions compressed; m small and crowded; P with hump to the left.

Superficiality

Inferior; garlands; concave t-bars; d ending in scroll; signature with wavy or curved underscore.

Susceptibility (Easily offended, flattered or influenced)

Very inclined; acutely inclined; round and light; angular above curved base line; concave t-bars; d with looped stem.

Tactfulness (Diplomacy)

Superior reclined; ovals carefully closed or semi-closed. Handwriting is neat, well ordered and well balanced. Words taper smaller at the end. Contributing factors are patience, intelligence, good balance. There is a shade of difference between tact which has a feeling of consideration and kindness) and 'diplomacy' (which can have ulterior motives). The diplomat may have a way or sineous base line in superior handwriting.

Tactlessness

Ovals wide open; narrow or no margins; hasty; post-placed t-bars; abrupt terminals; words enlarge towards end. Contributing factors are lack of discipline, of intelligence, of balance; emotionalism and an explosive nature.

Tenacity

Angular; very firm, even pressure; strong and hooked t-bars; t-looped for the cross; downturned hook on finals; prolonged finals descending and dub-shaped; S tied to following letter; S ending in loop below base line.

Timidity

Very small; light; weak t-bars; inferior handwriting with excessively short-t-bars; pre-placed i-dots; capitals no higher than small letters; compressed upper loops; m small and crowded; P hump to left of stem.

Undisciplined (Restlessness, Waywardness)

Constantly changing slant; varying base line; very large; badly spaced; hasty.

Vacillation

Irregular form; slant, base line, speed, pressure and margins varying; preplaced weak of concave t-bars.

Versatility

The small letters appearing in varied forms; changing slant and size; broken letter connections; uneven margins.

Violence (Brutality)

Heavy; muddy; smeary; t-bars long and too heavy; t-bars heavy and descending; t-bars thin to-think; finals heavy, descending and pointed or descending and dub-shaped ascending and dub-shaped.

Vitality (Dynamism, Vigor)

Very large; firm and heavy; rapid; long, heavy t-bars; heavy or many exclamation points; long lower extensions; M final abrupt.

Vivacity (Animation, Gaiety)

Supple, ascending base line; very large or large; fast; long thin t-bars; crack-the-whip t-bars; i-dots high and dashed or crescent-shaped; elongated commas; wavy beginning strokes; L descending curved ending; tall upper extension on p; p a single stroke; p made in a single, simple stroke; s taller than other middle long letters; S comma like figures fluent.

Vulgarity (Bad Taste)

Ugly forms; badly spaced; illegible; narrow or no margins; pressure exaggerated and muddy; up and down strokes equally heavy; or ornate, ungraceful capitals; base loop of L enlarged; M middle hump highest; ungainly preportioned M; middle stroke of M plunging downward.

Will Power

Angular ; firm; strong pressure; strong regular t-bars made like crosses; decisive strokes; abrupt finals; angular m; signature final in form of zig-zag.

GRAPHOLOGY HANDWRITING ANALYSIS

JOHN GILLMAN